Le Beau Ideal

Brandy Lindsey

ISBN: 0615729290
ISBN-13: 978-0615729299

DEDICATION

For Paula, my other mother, and Mad and Rob.

The Definition of Beauty is
That Definition is none—
Of Heaven, easing Analysis,
Since Heaven and He are one.

Emily Dickinson

ACKNOWLEDGMENTS

Many, many thanks to Frances Law, Paula Frye, William Paul Carter, Loretta Thompson, Joe Carr, Melissa McGuire, David Deal, Shannon Sharpensteen, Timmy Thompson, and the rest of the staff at Kentucky Down Under.

Autumn

Autumn, the year's last, loveliest smile.

William Cullen Bryant

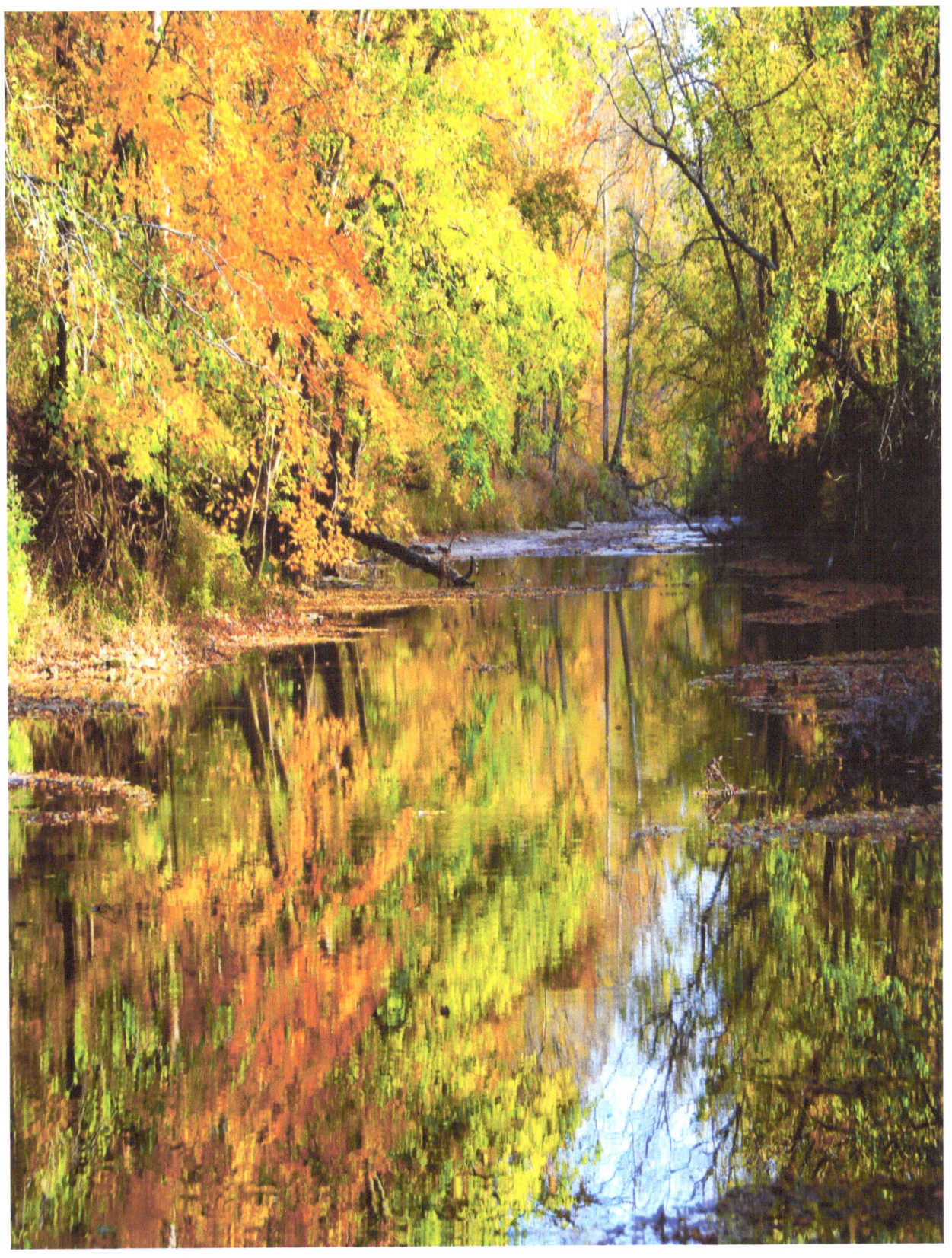

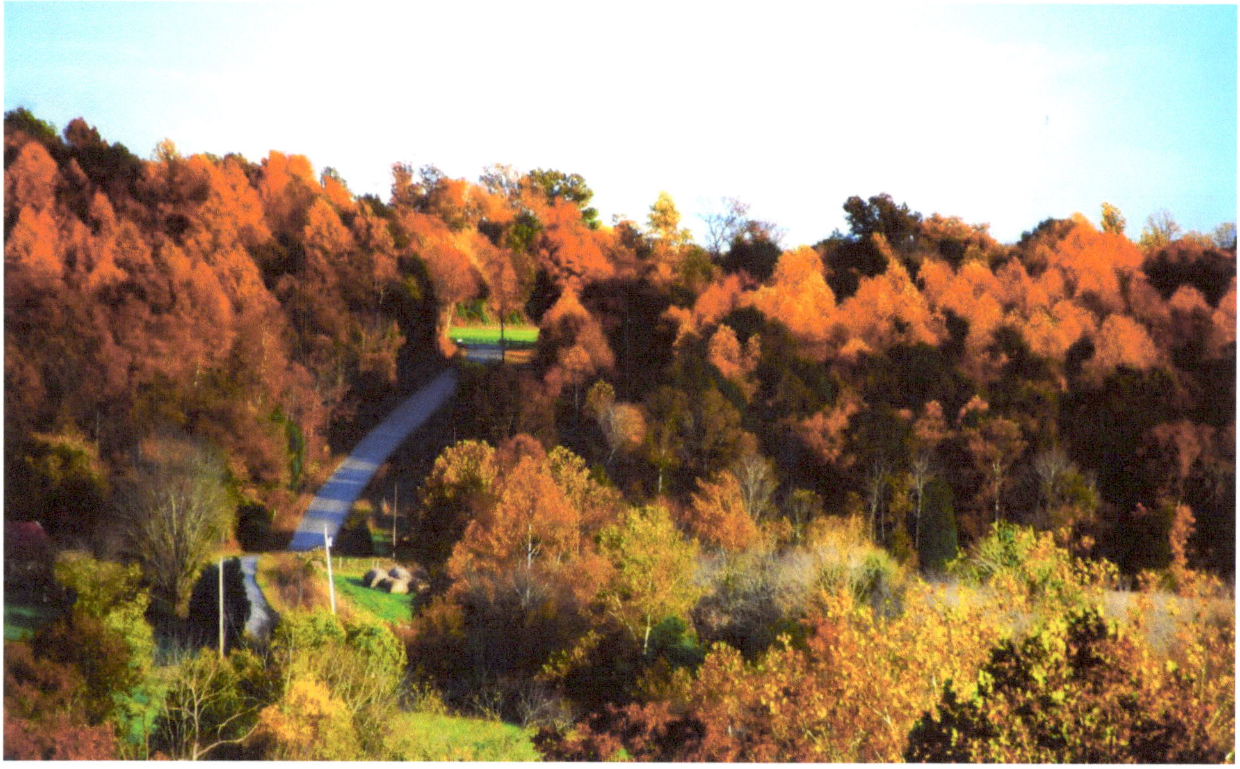

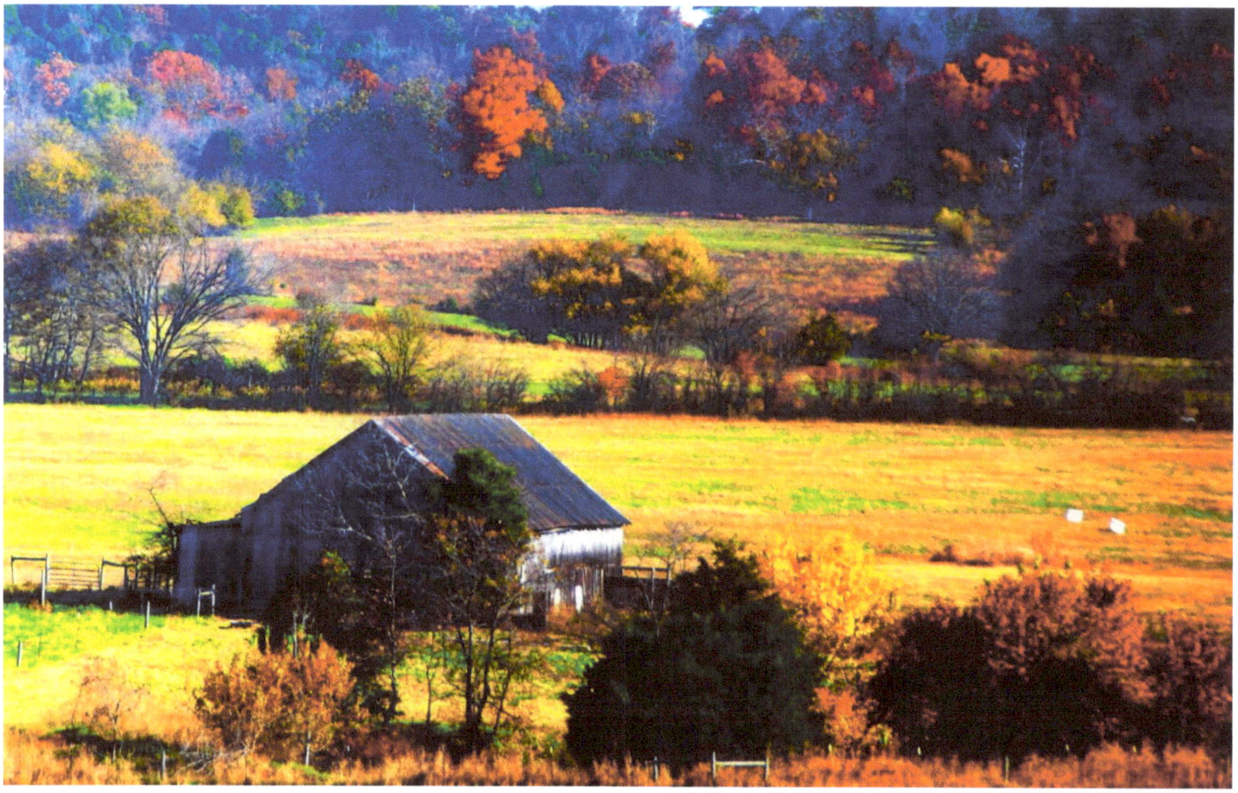

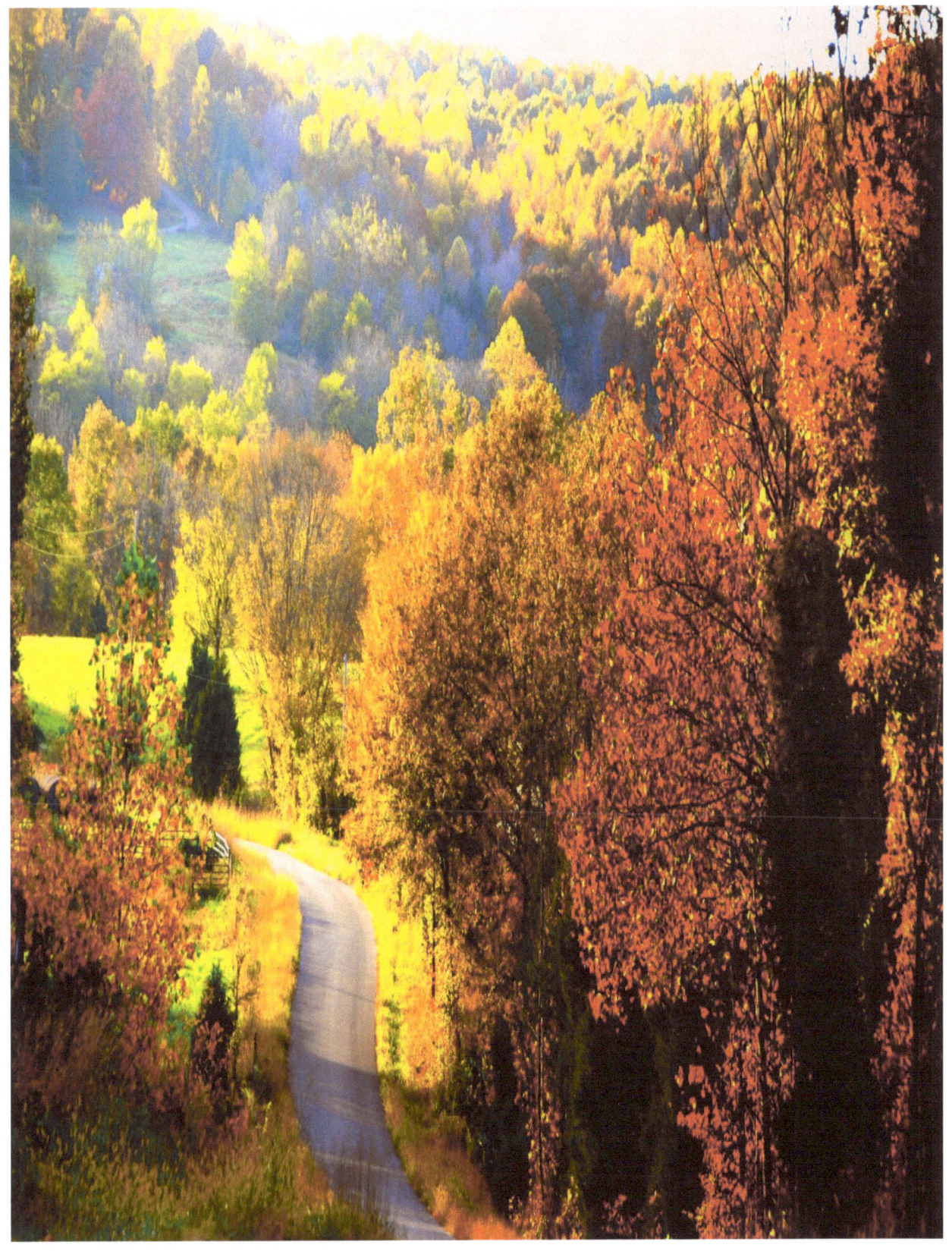

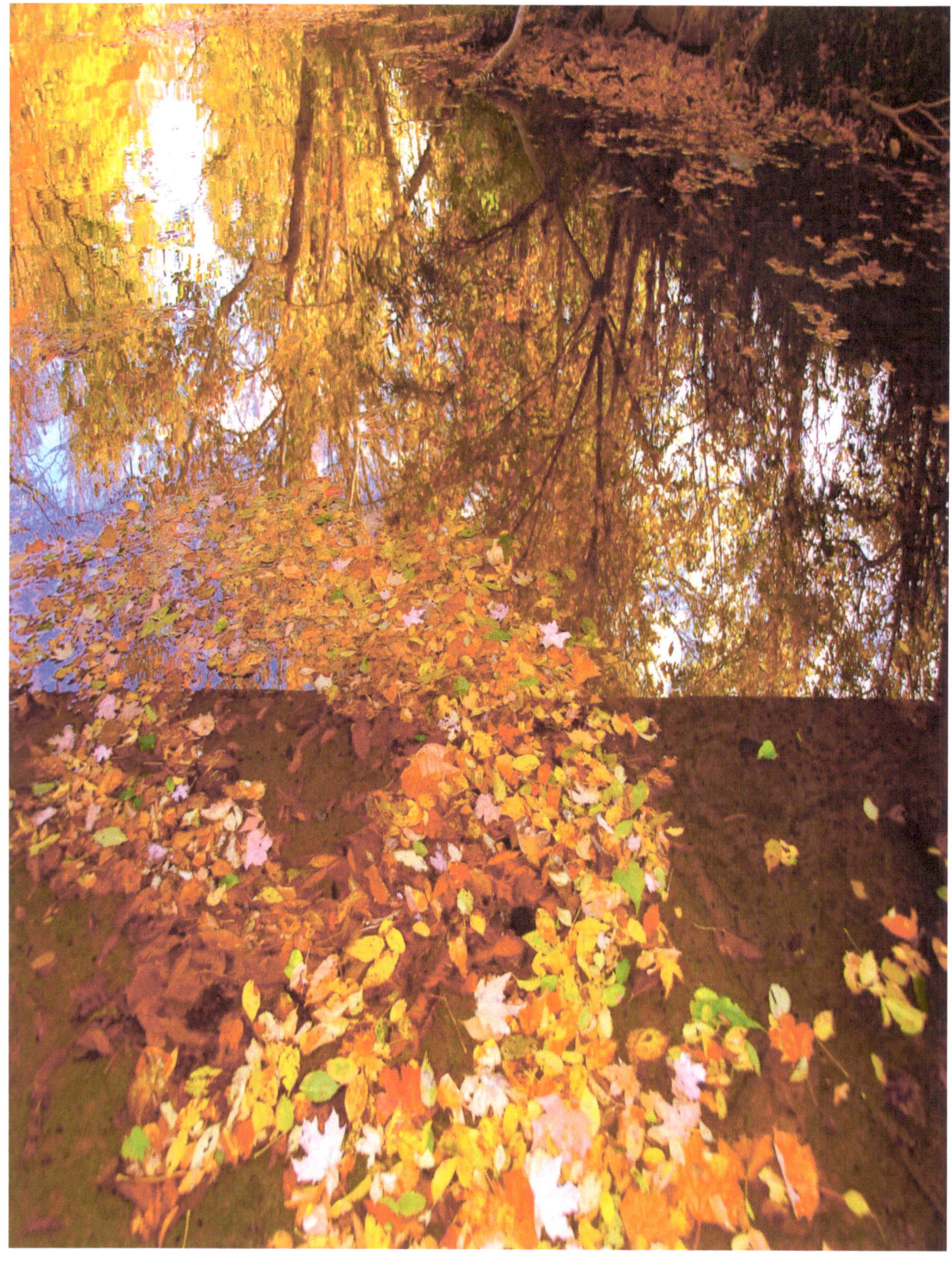

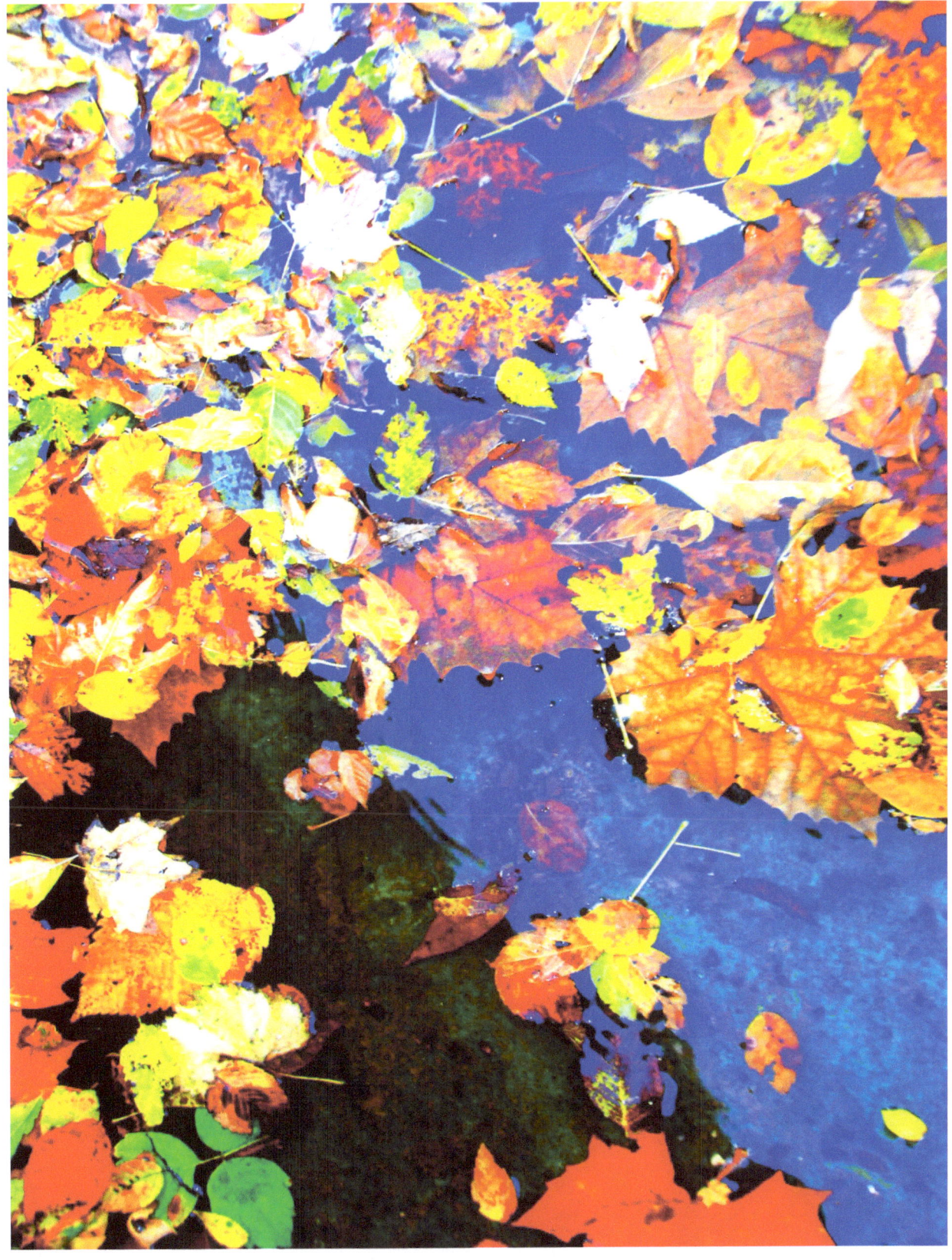

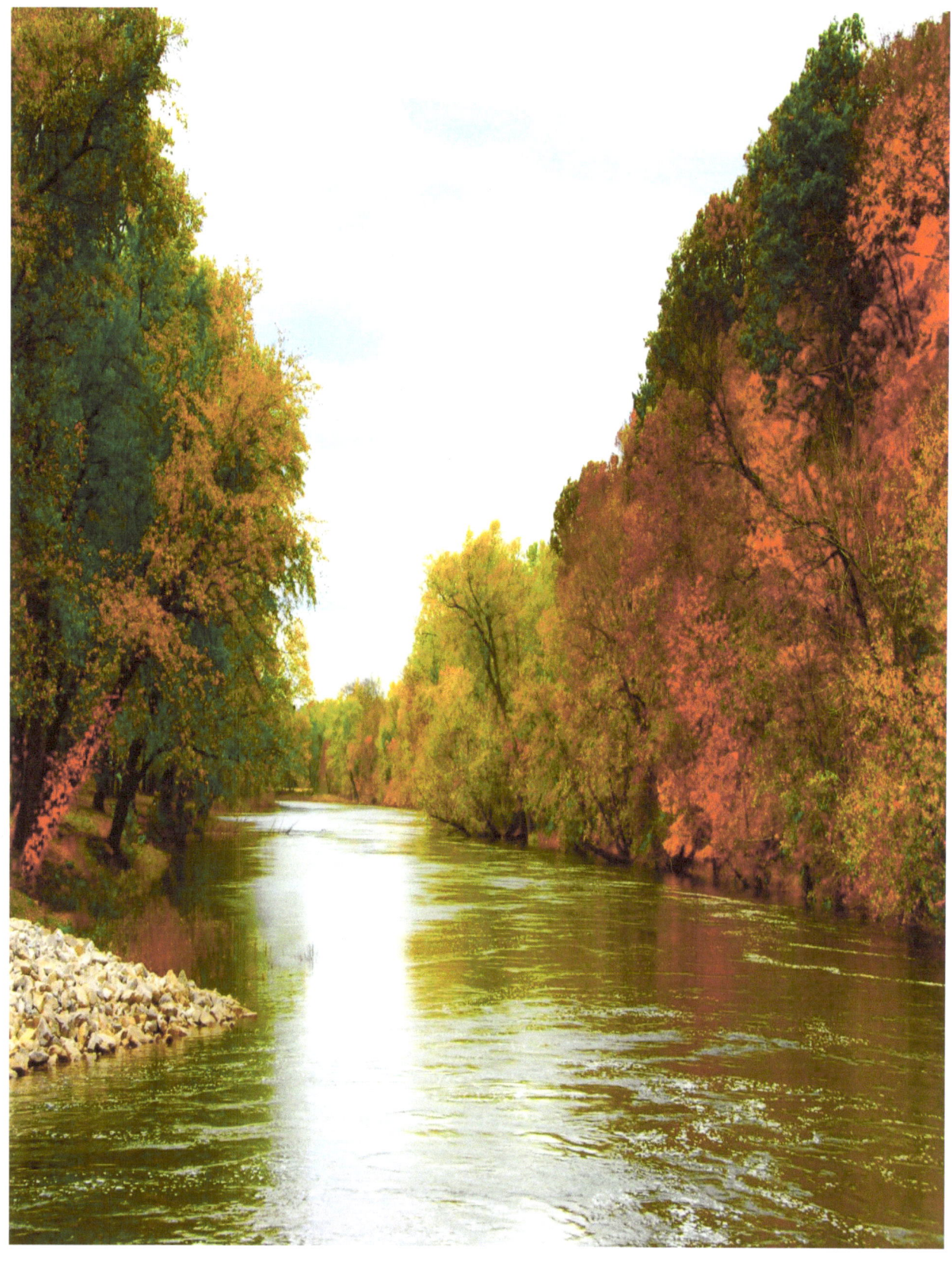

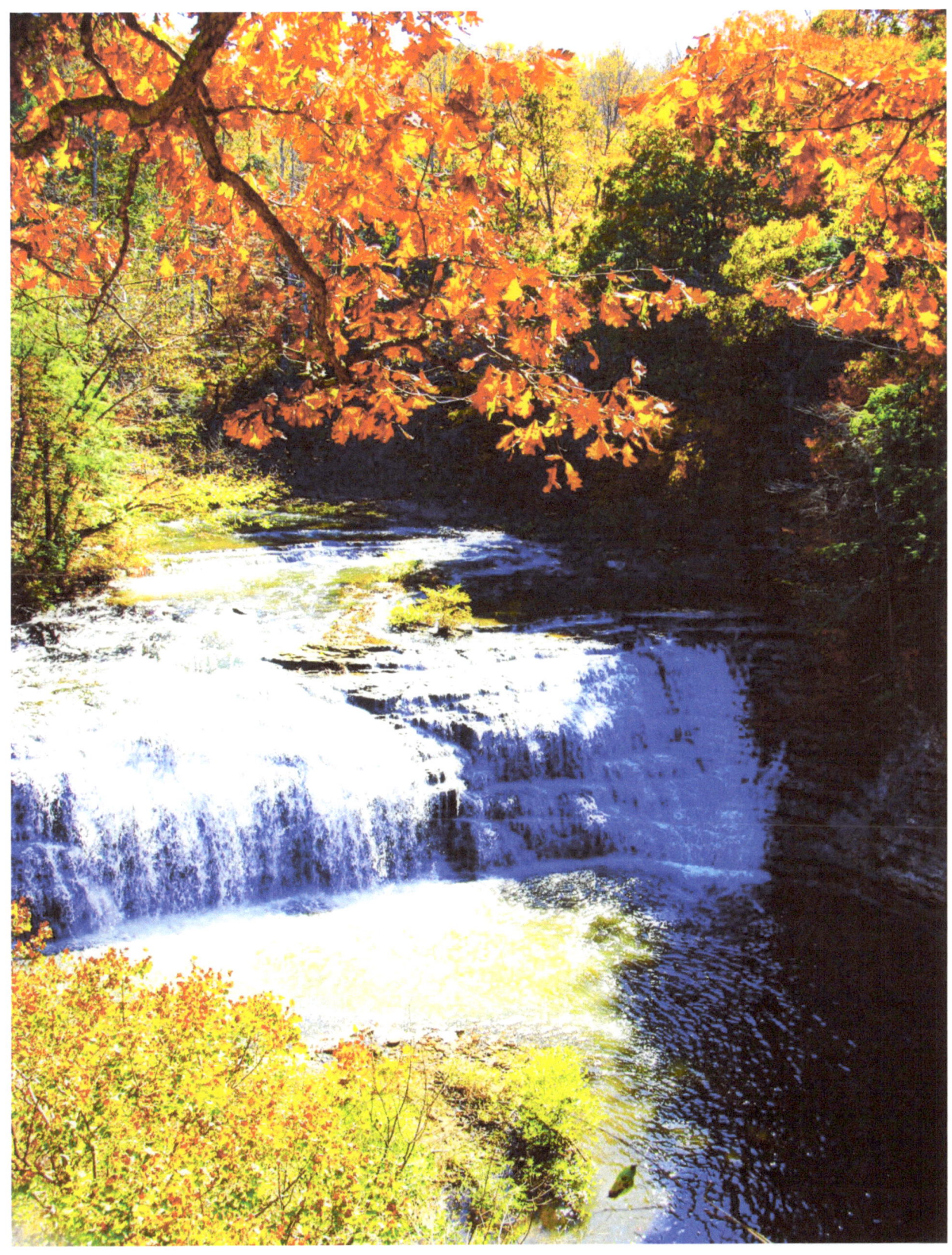

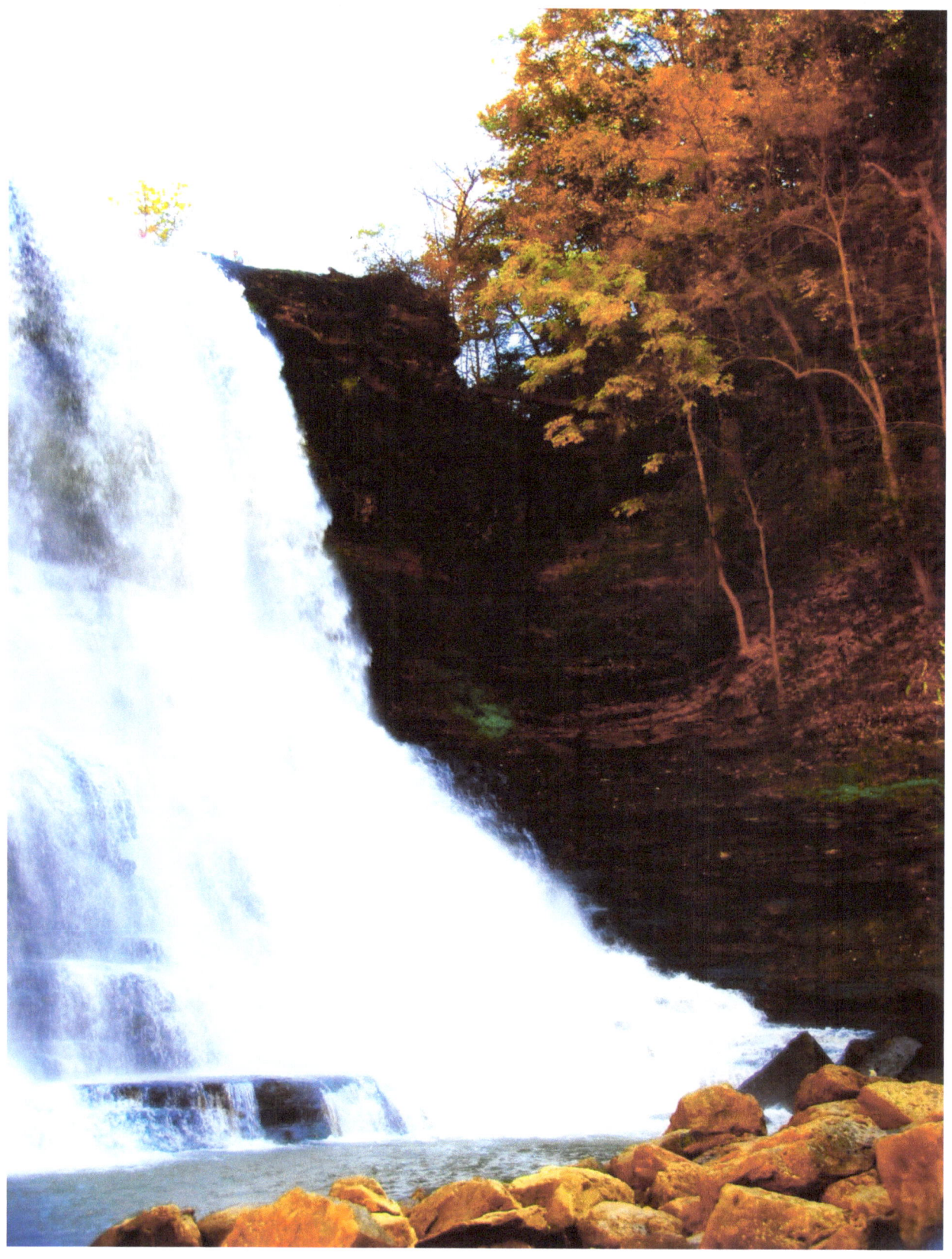

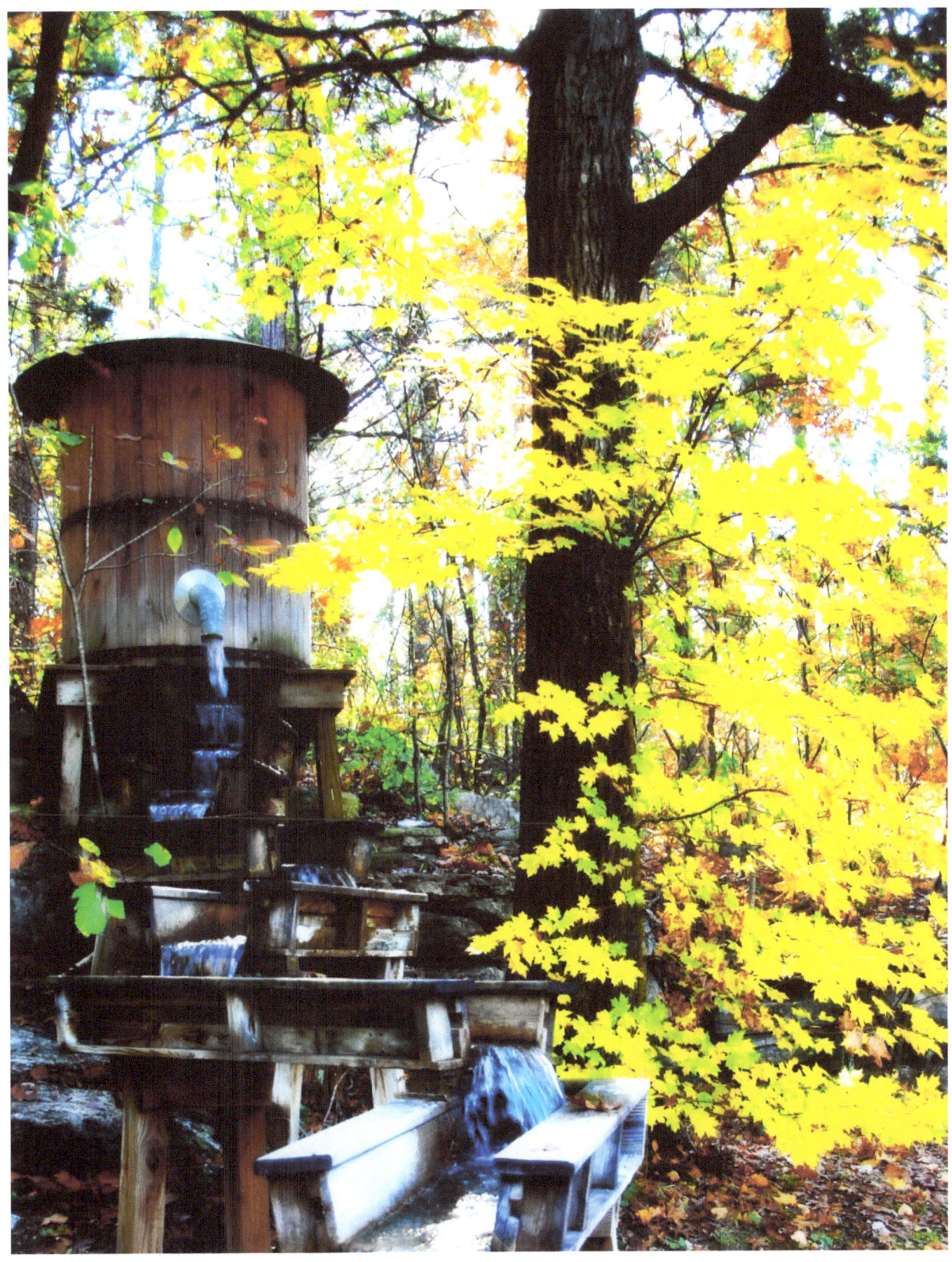

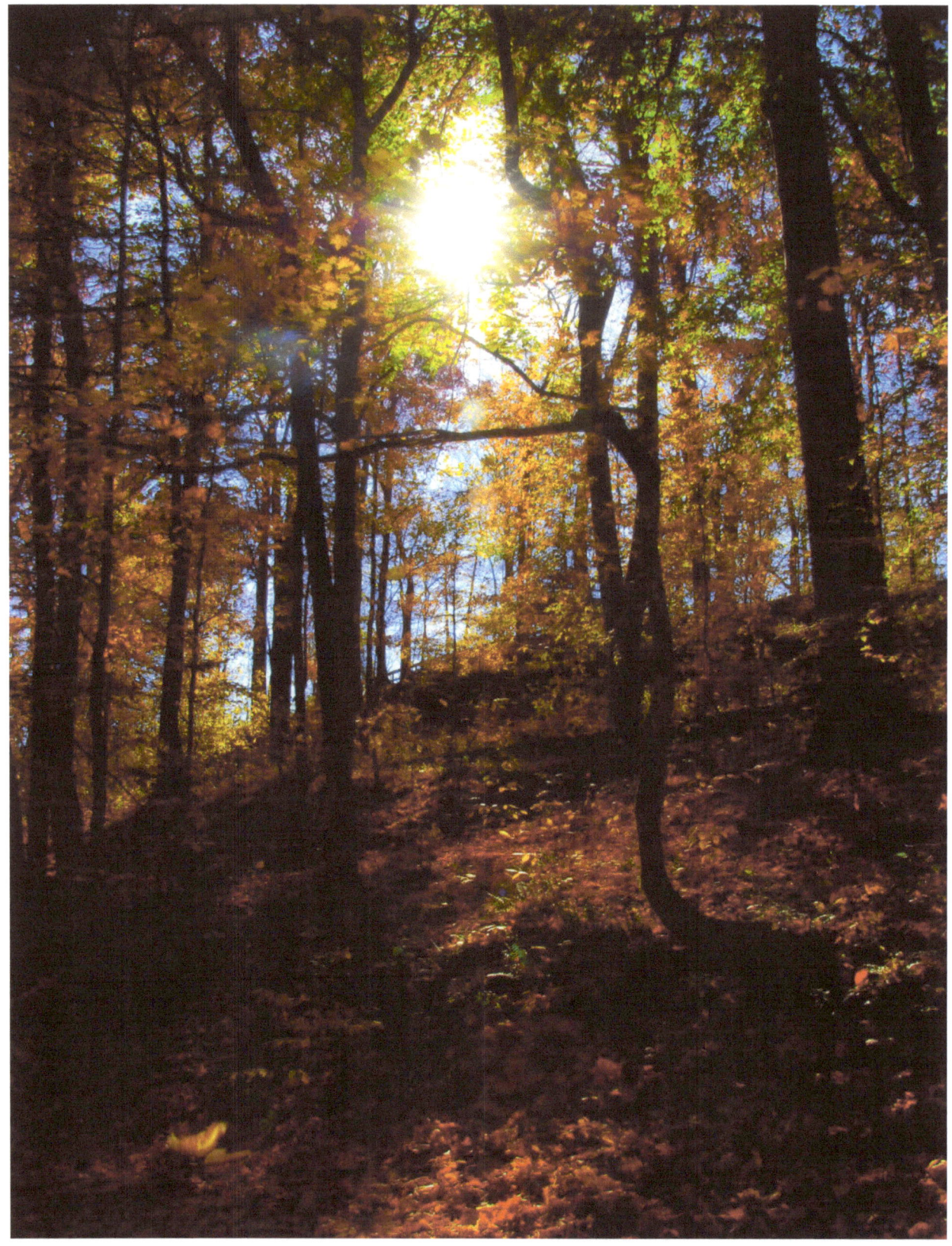

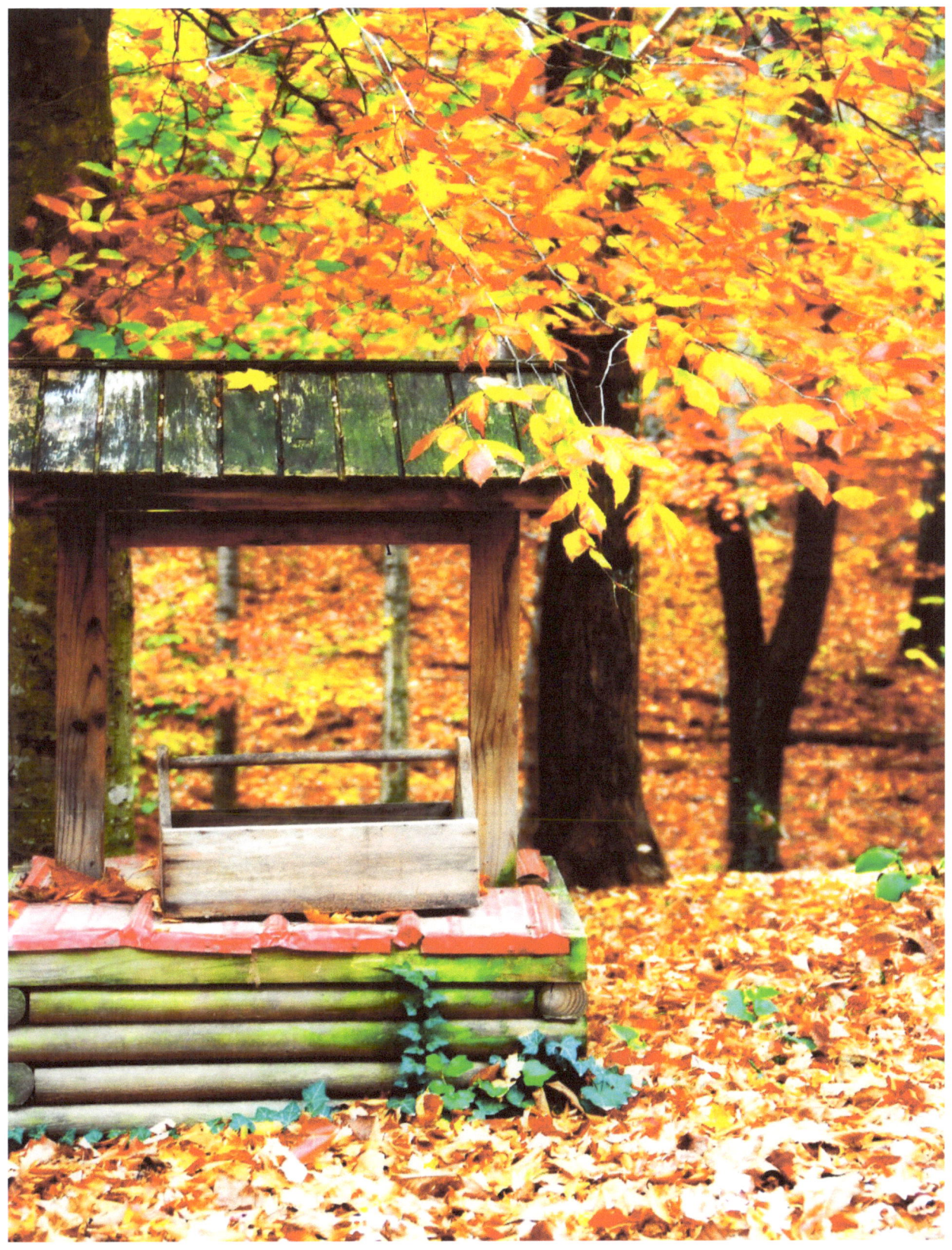

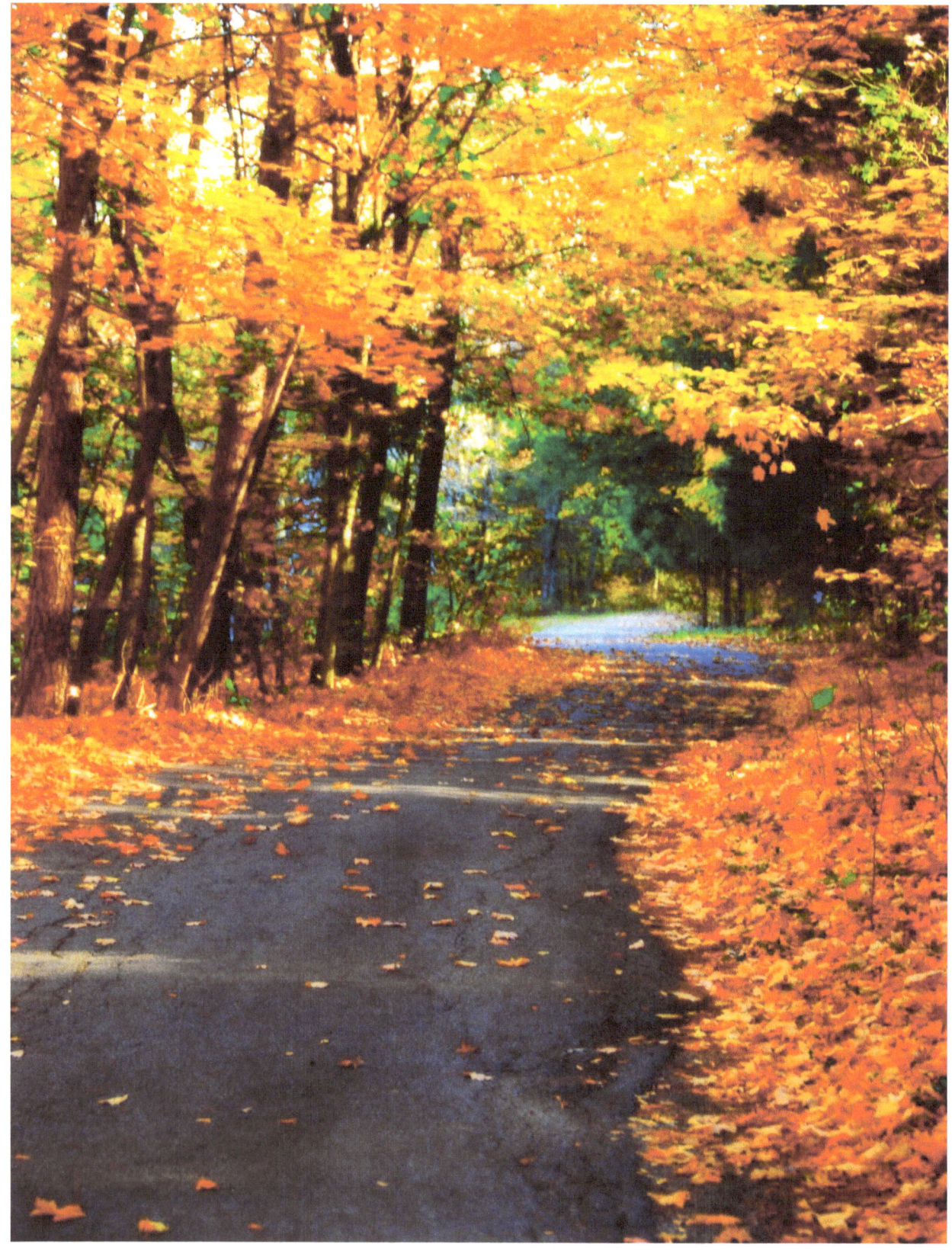

Lakeside Ladderback

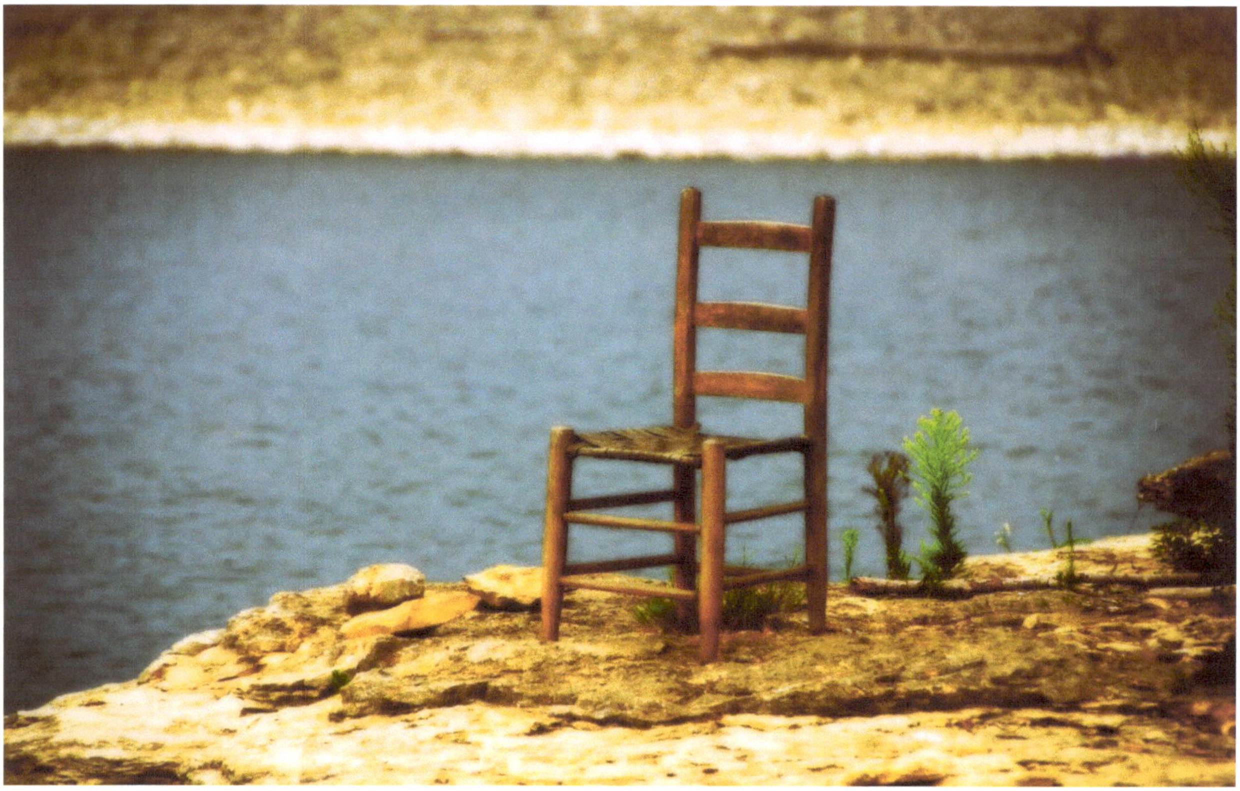

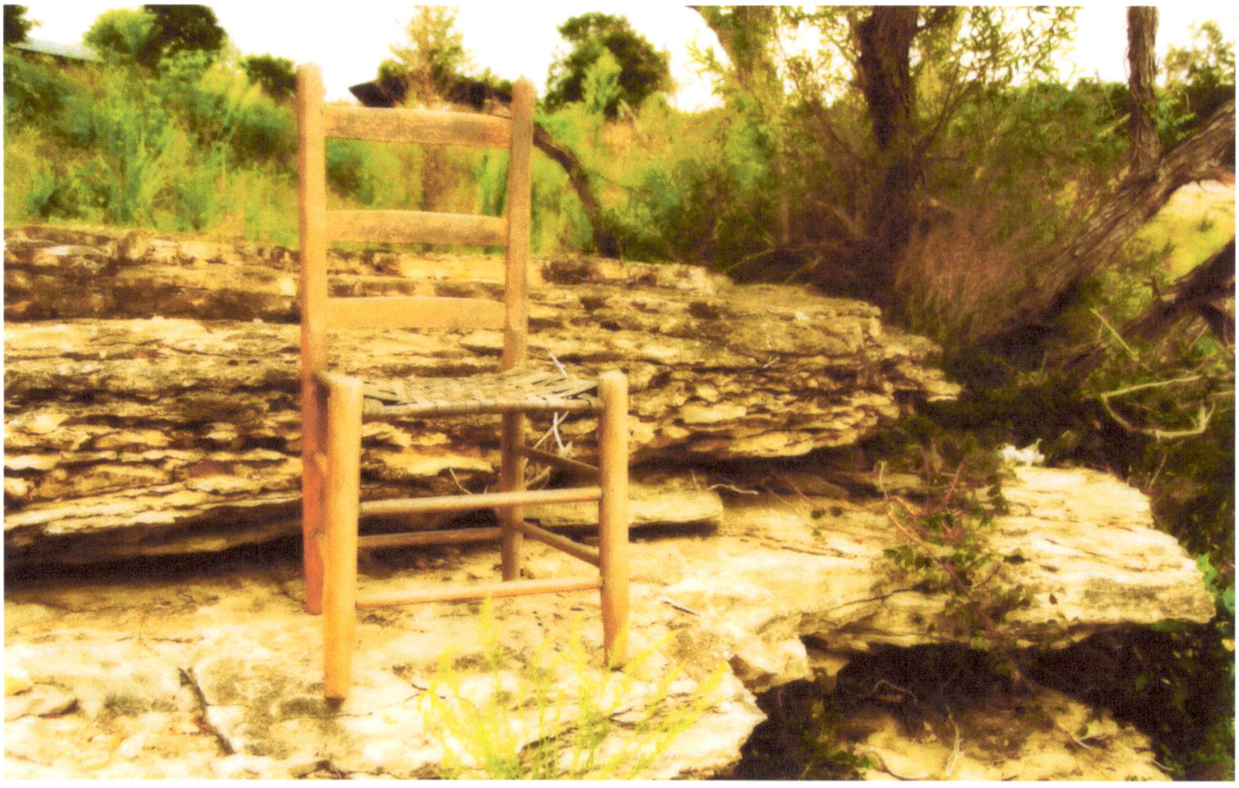

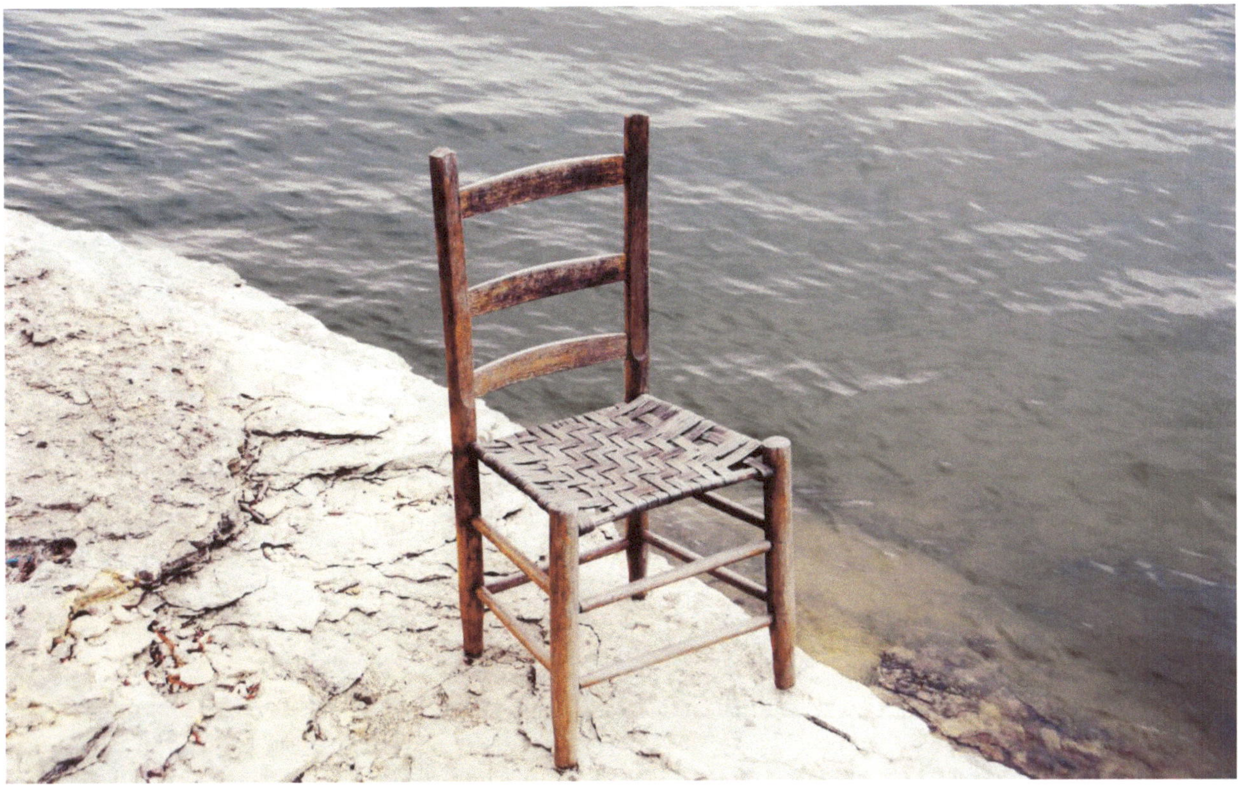

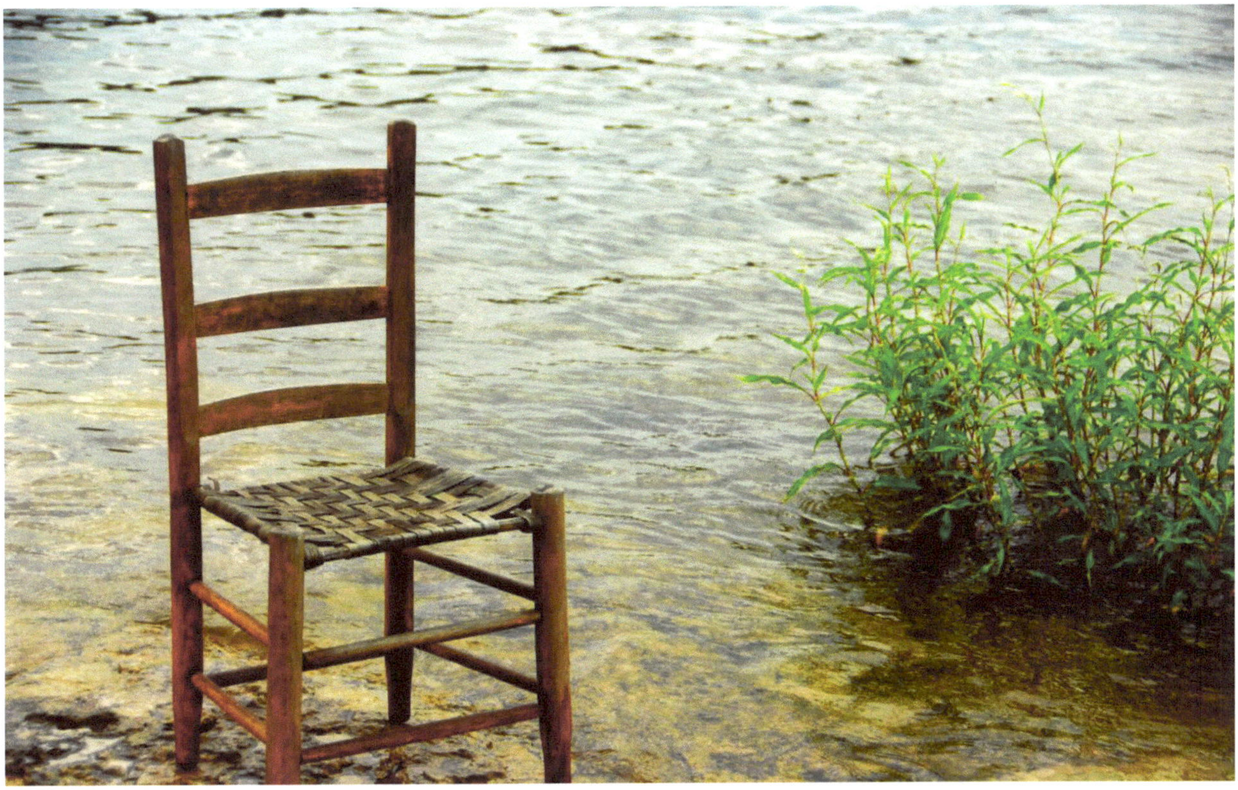

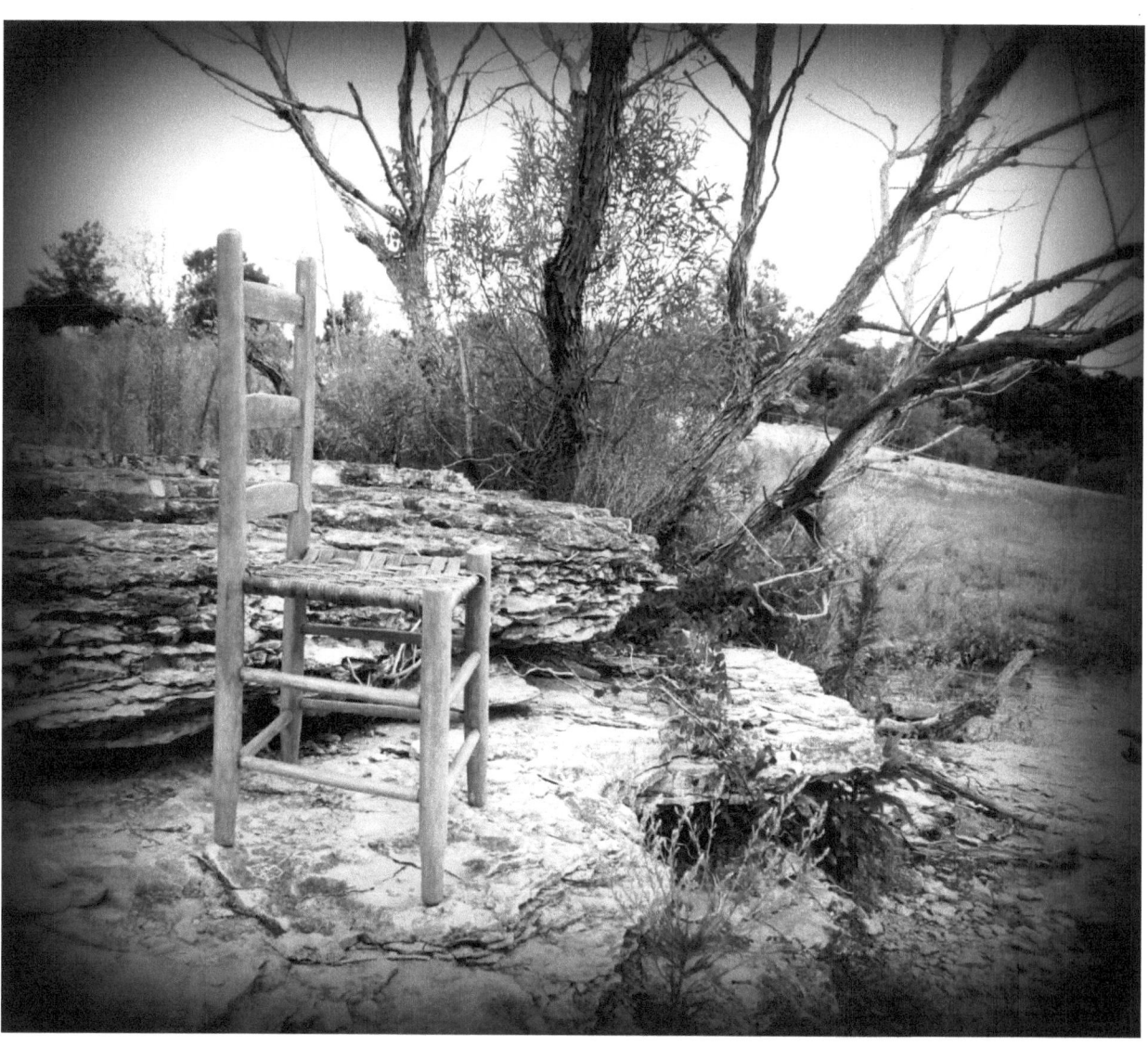

Paul in Repose

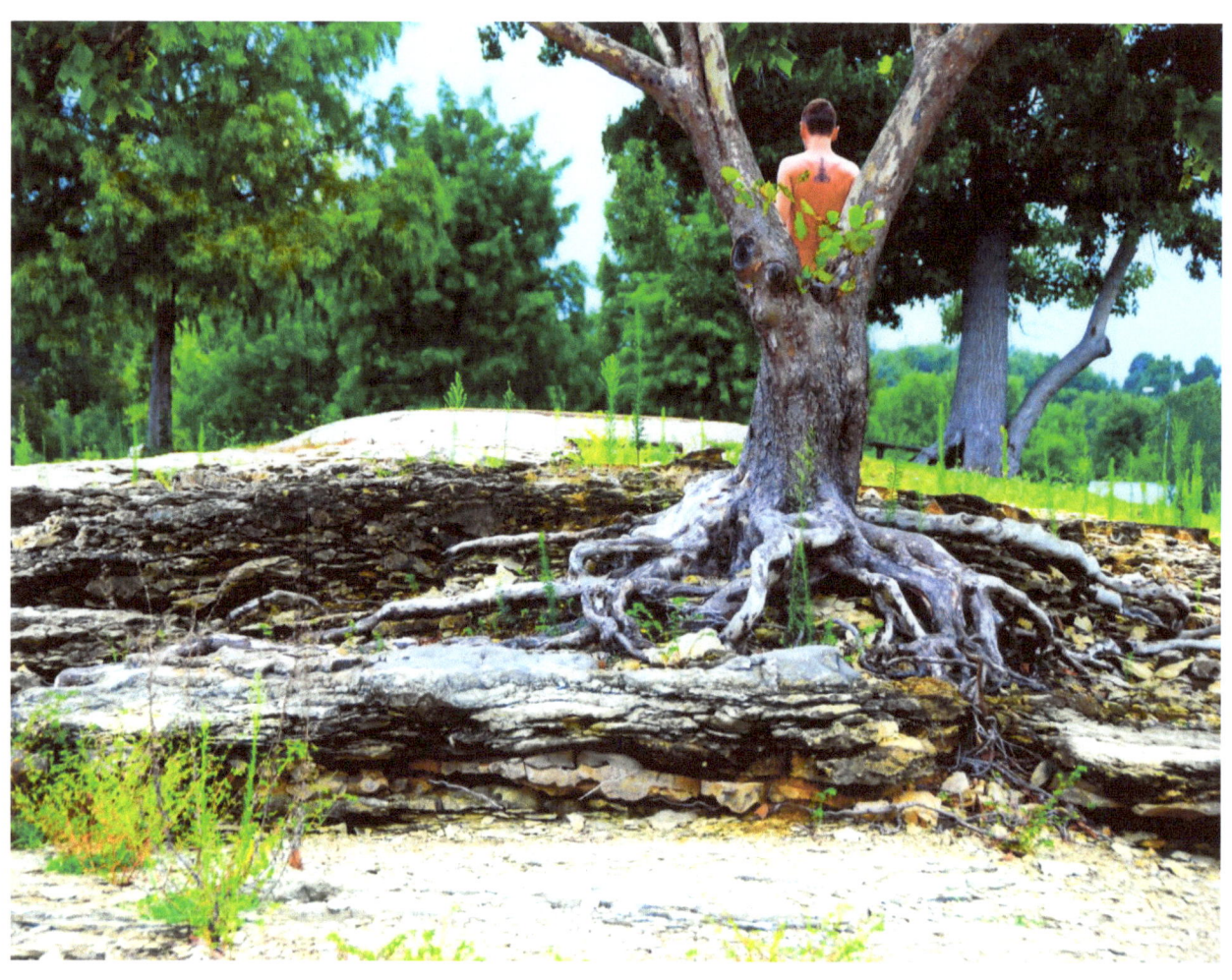

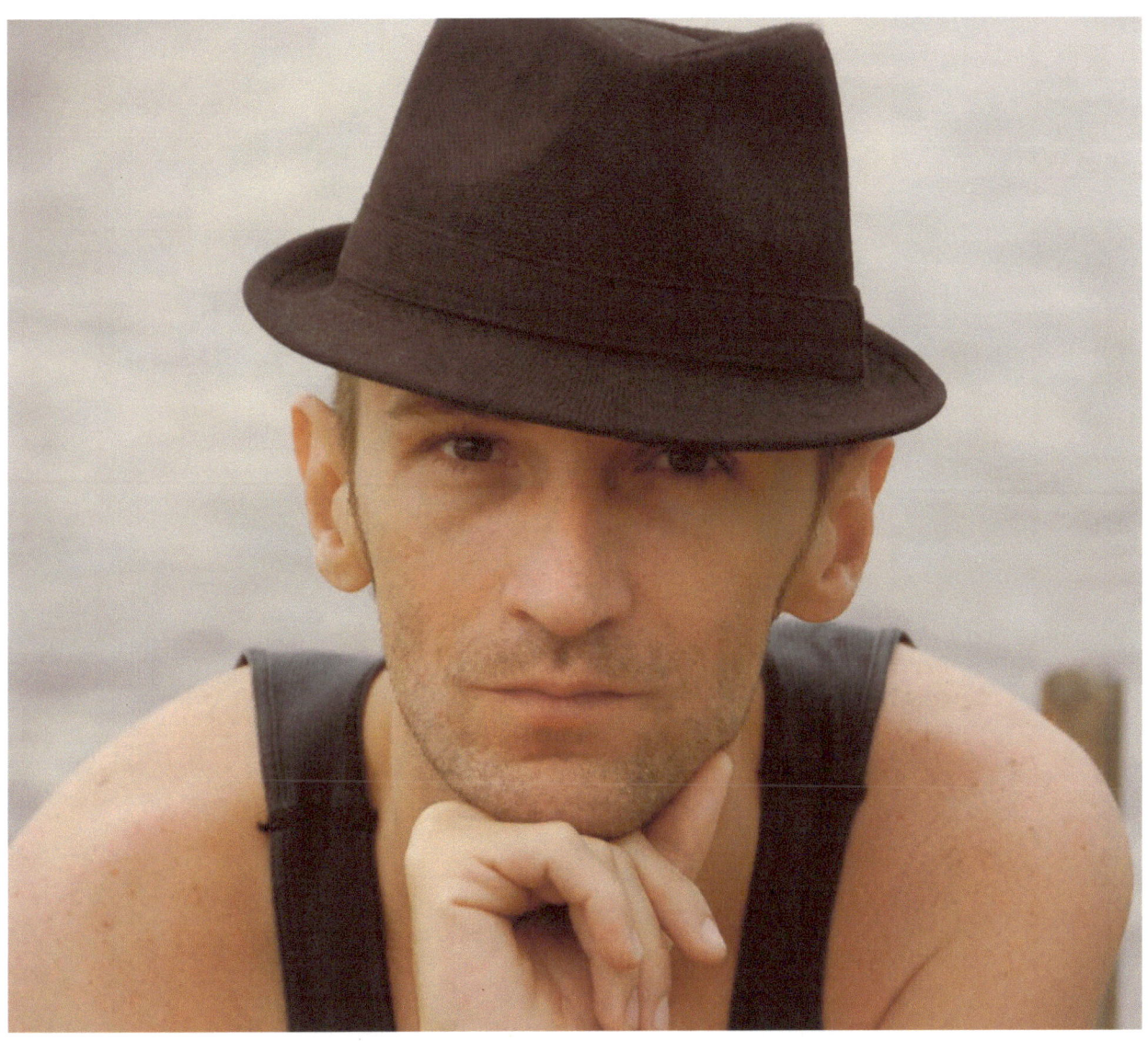

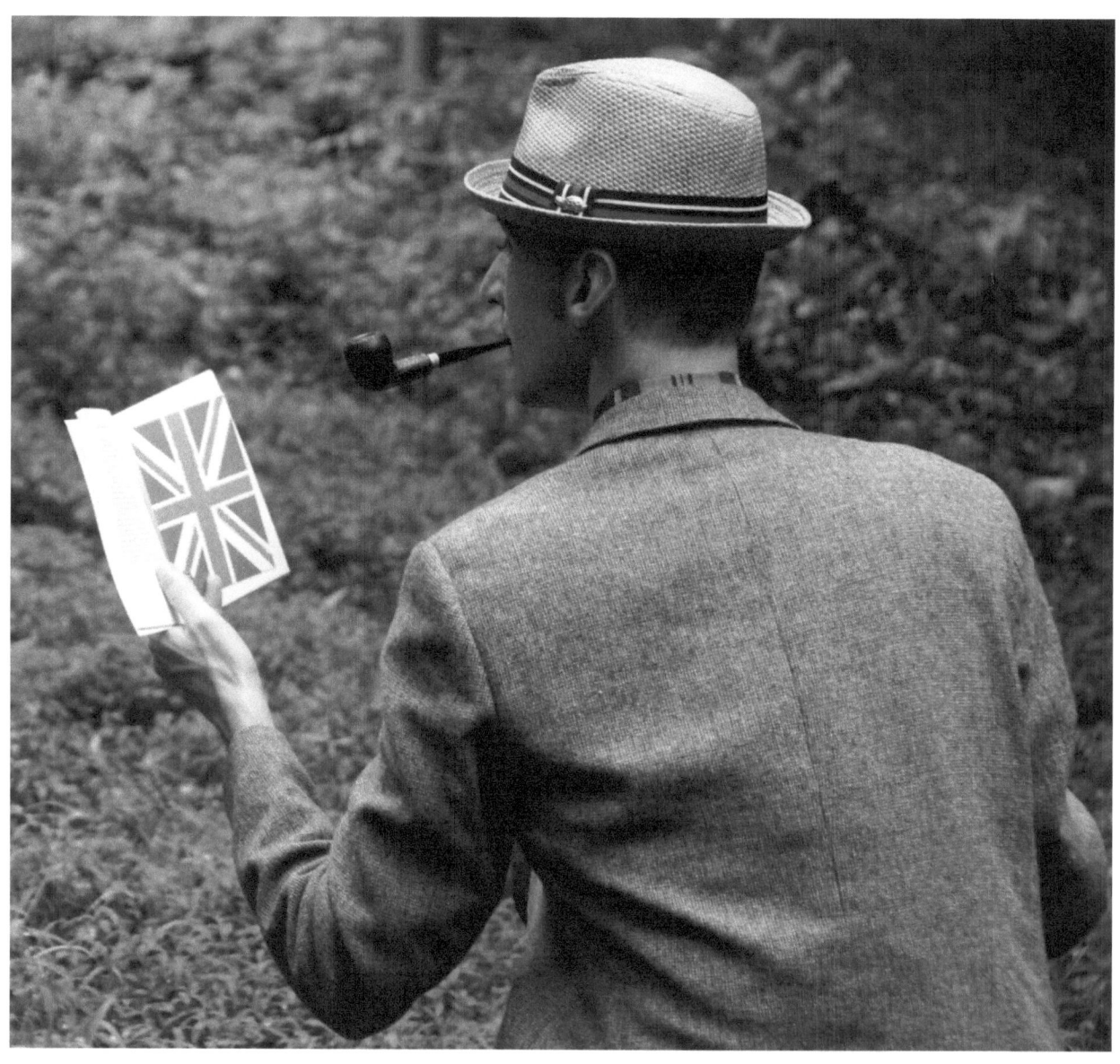

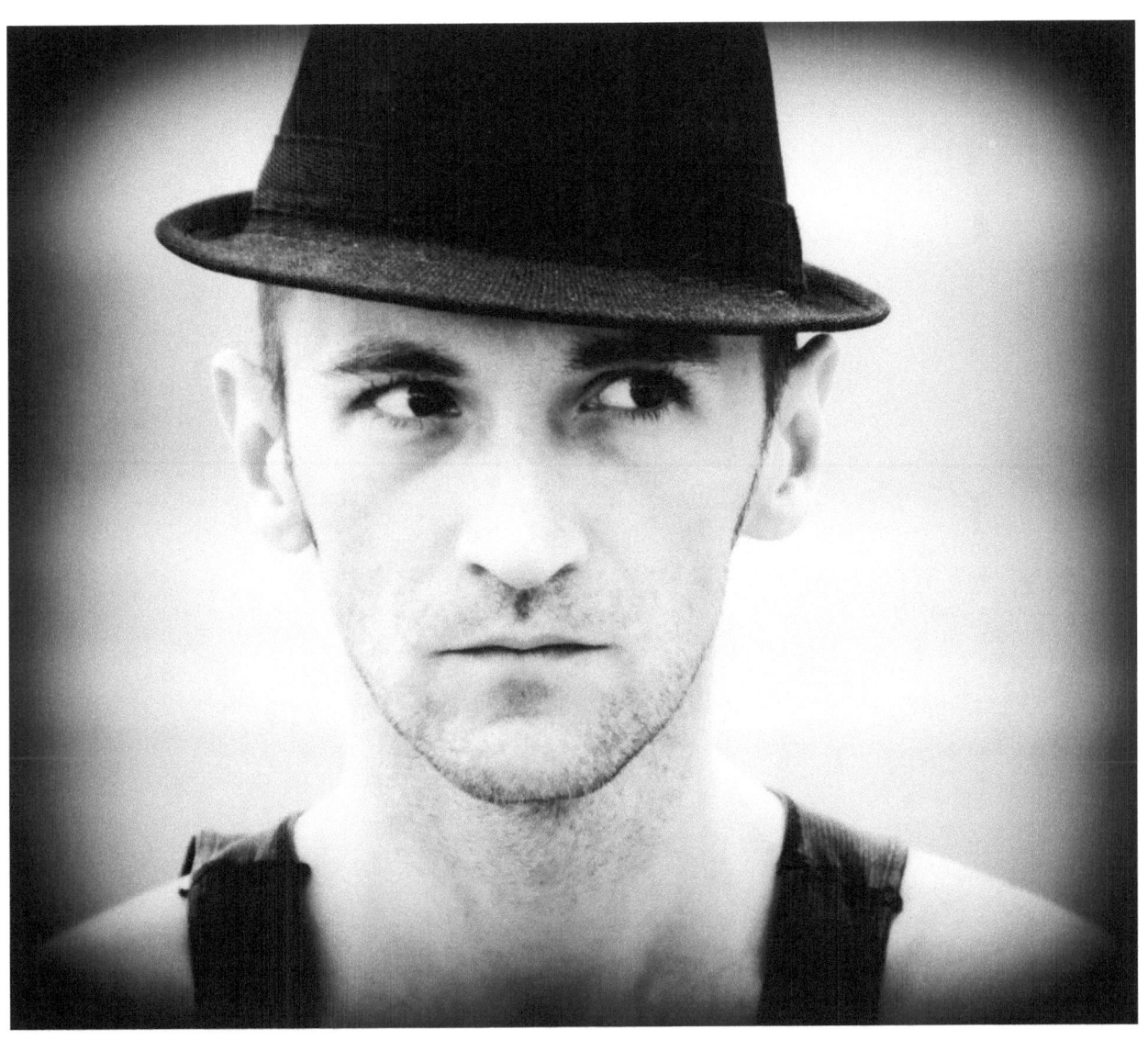

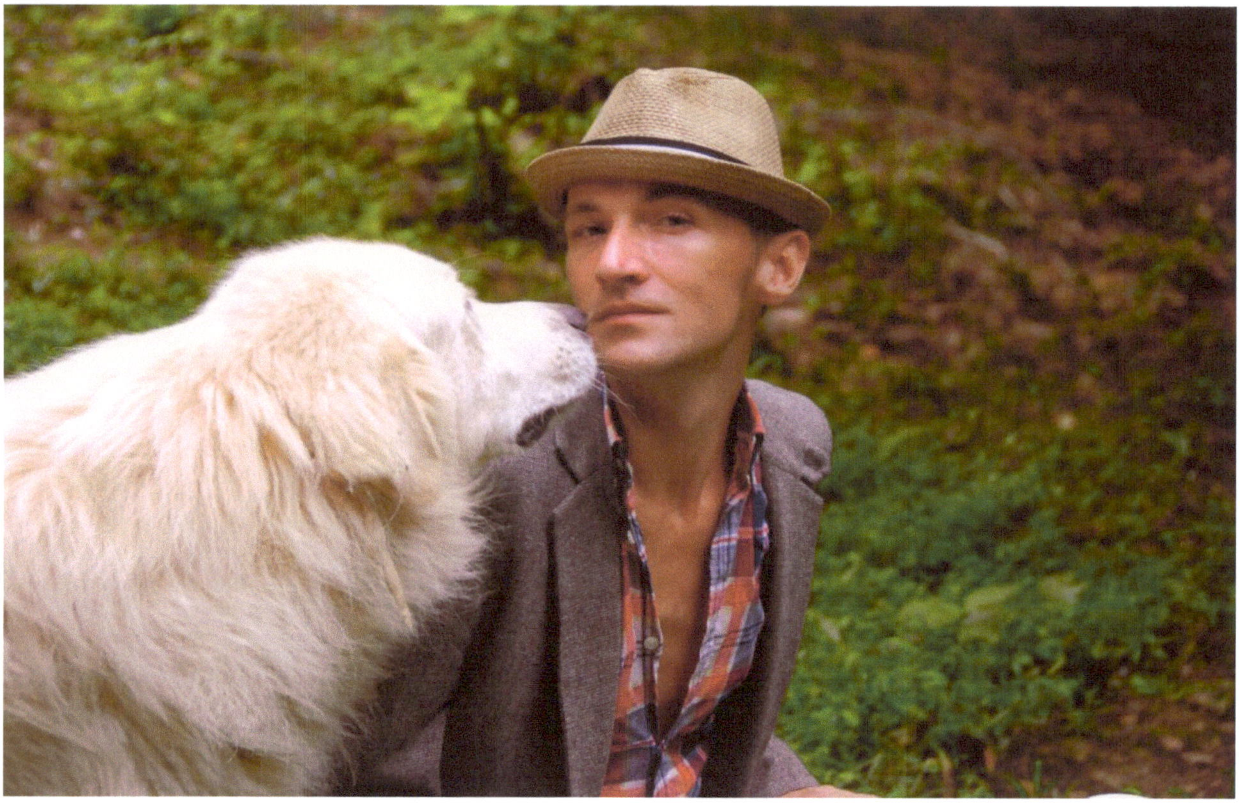

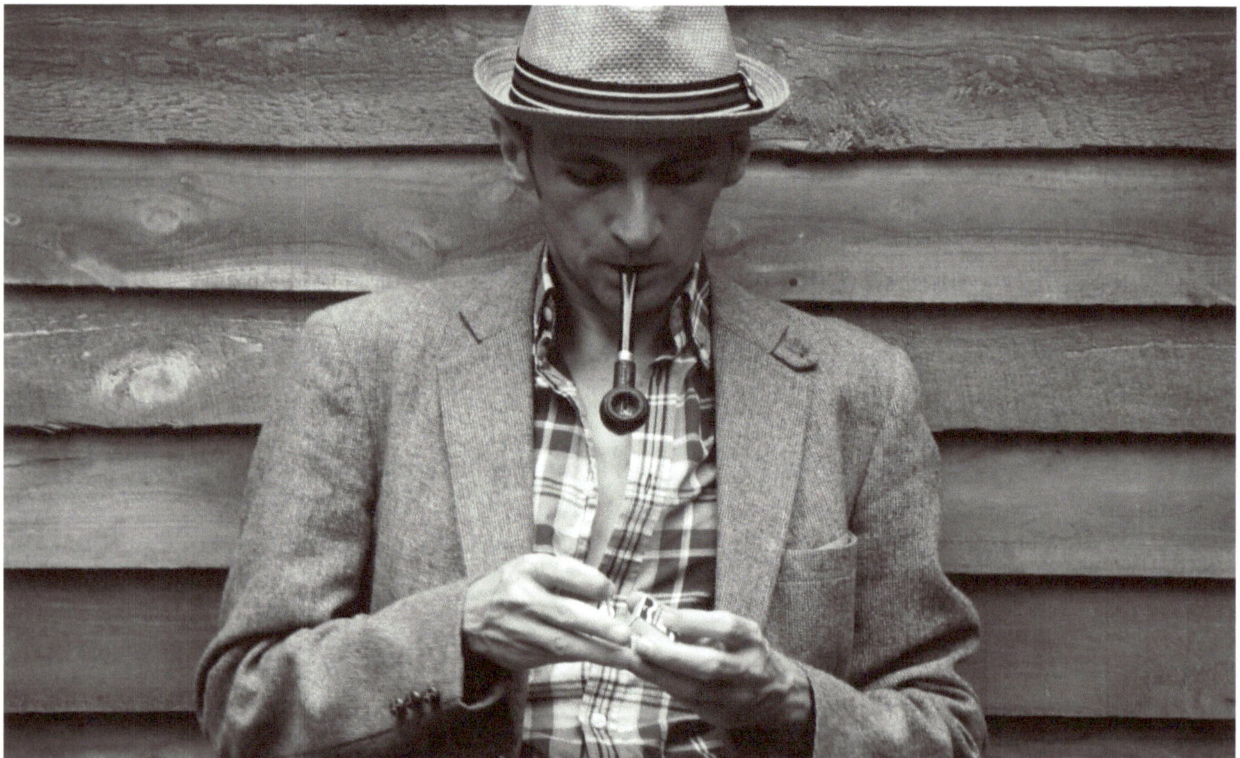

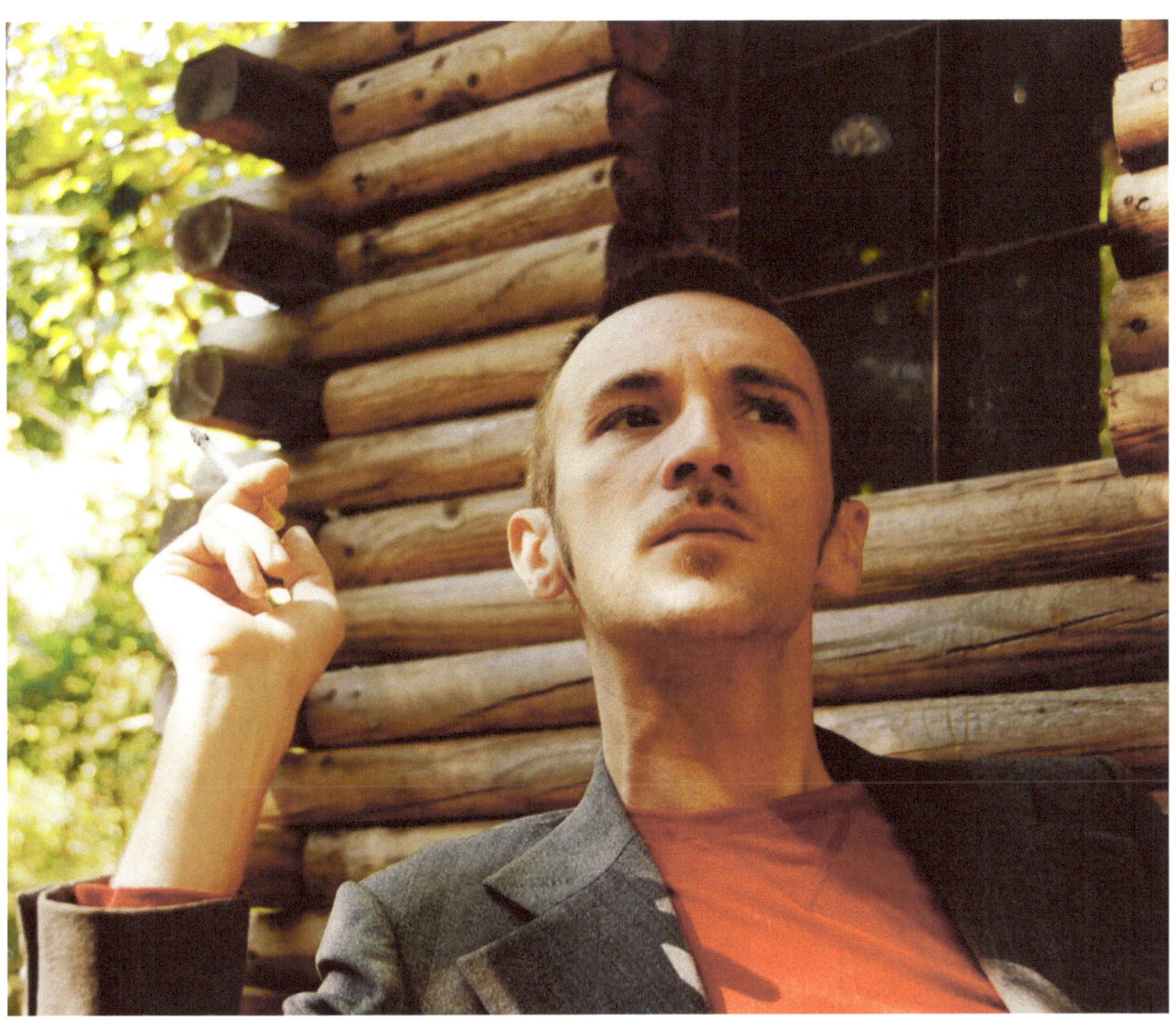

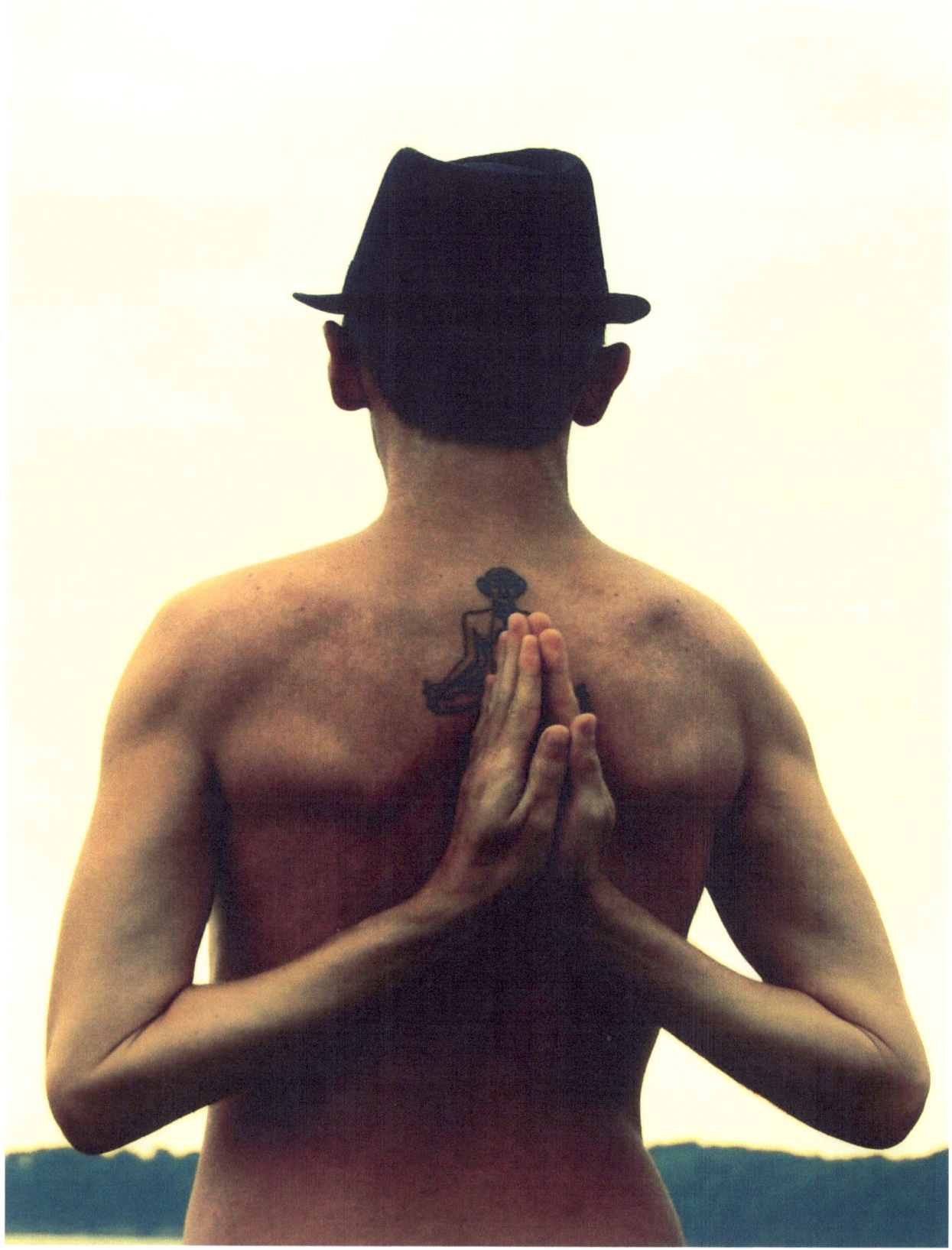

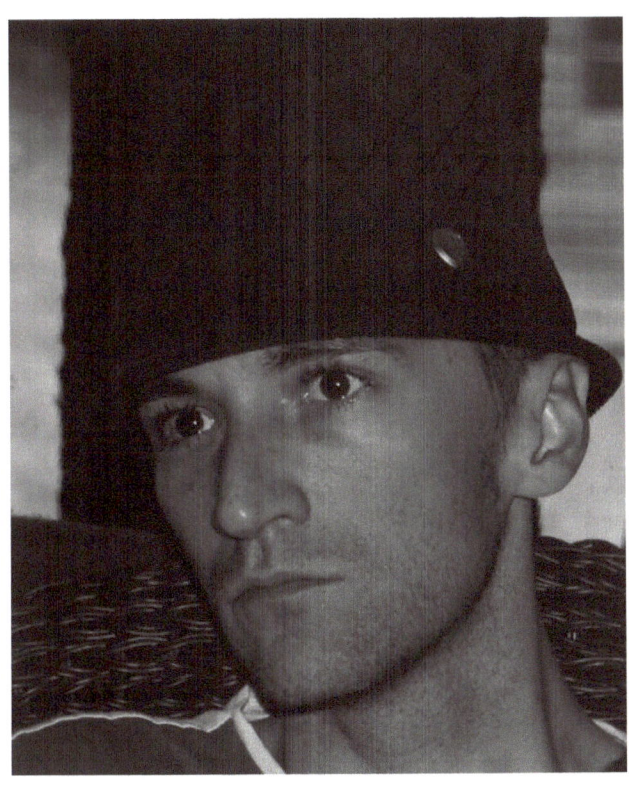

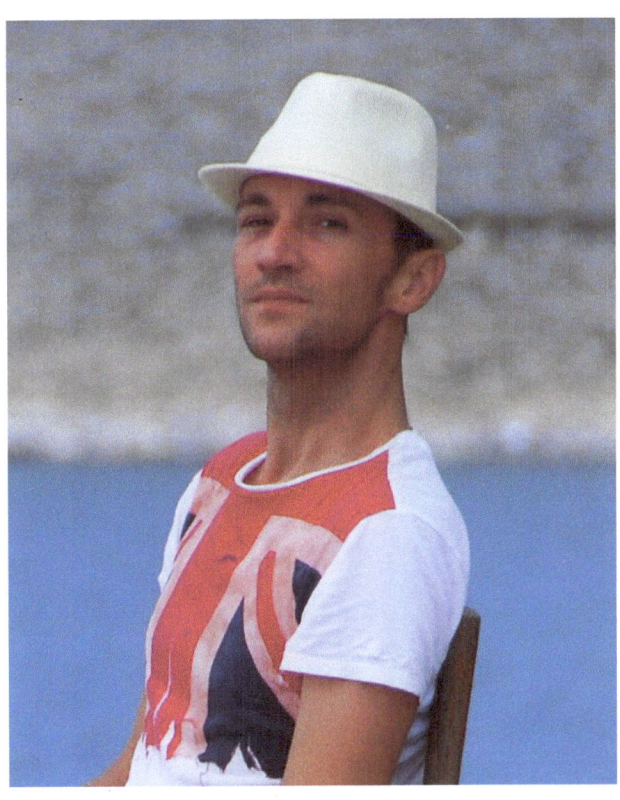

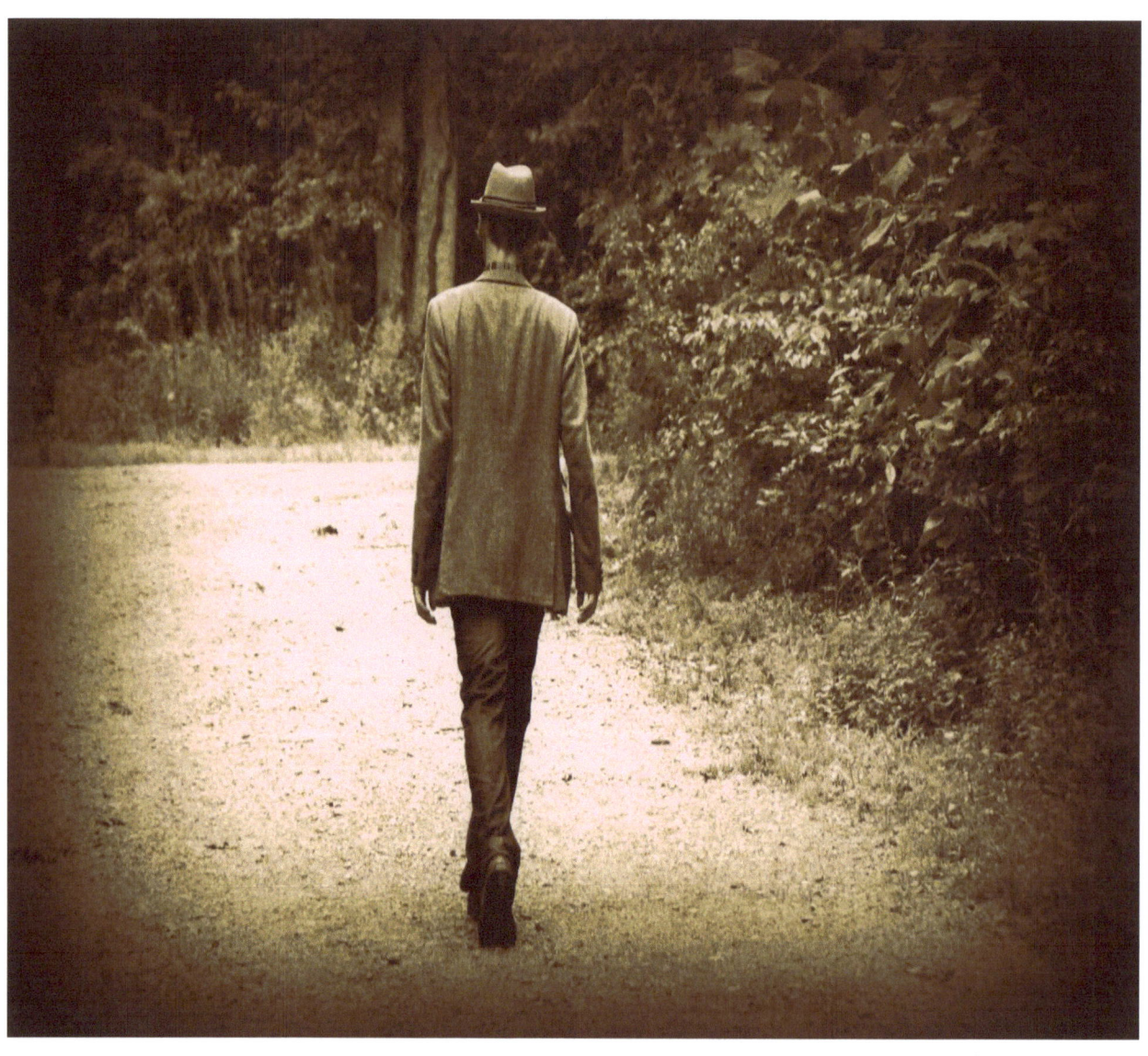

This and That

Trees

I think that I shall never see
A poem lovely as a tree.
A tree whose hungry mouth is pressed
Against the earth's sweet flowing breast;
A tree that looks at God all day
And lifts her leafy arms to pray;
A tree that may in summer wear
A nest of robins in her hair;
Upon whose bosom snow has lain;
Who intimately lives with rain.
Poems are written by fools like me,
But only God can make a tree.

Joyce Kilmer

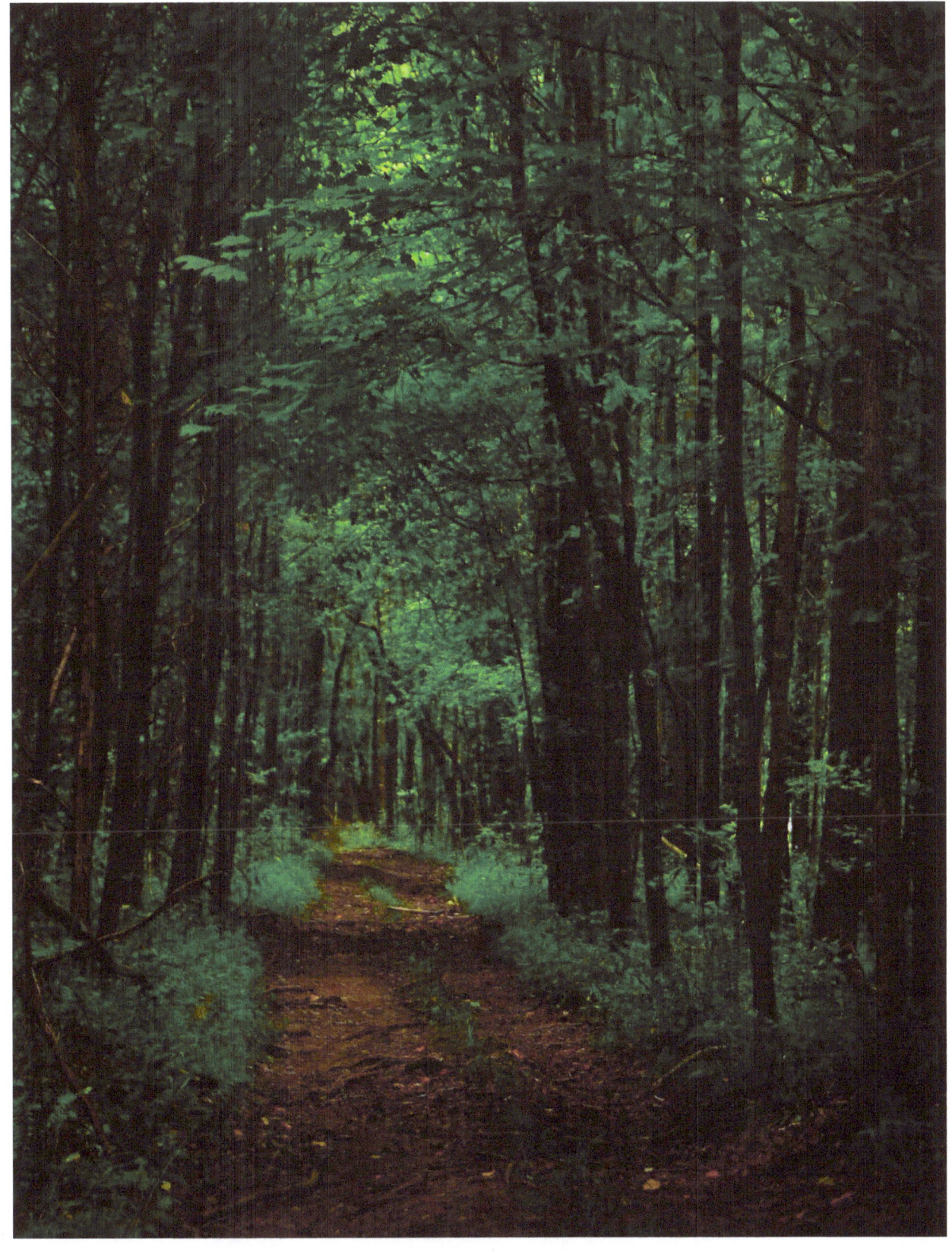

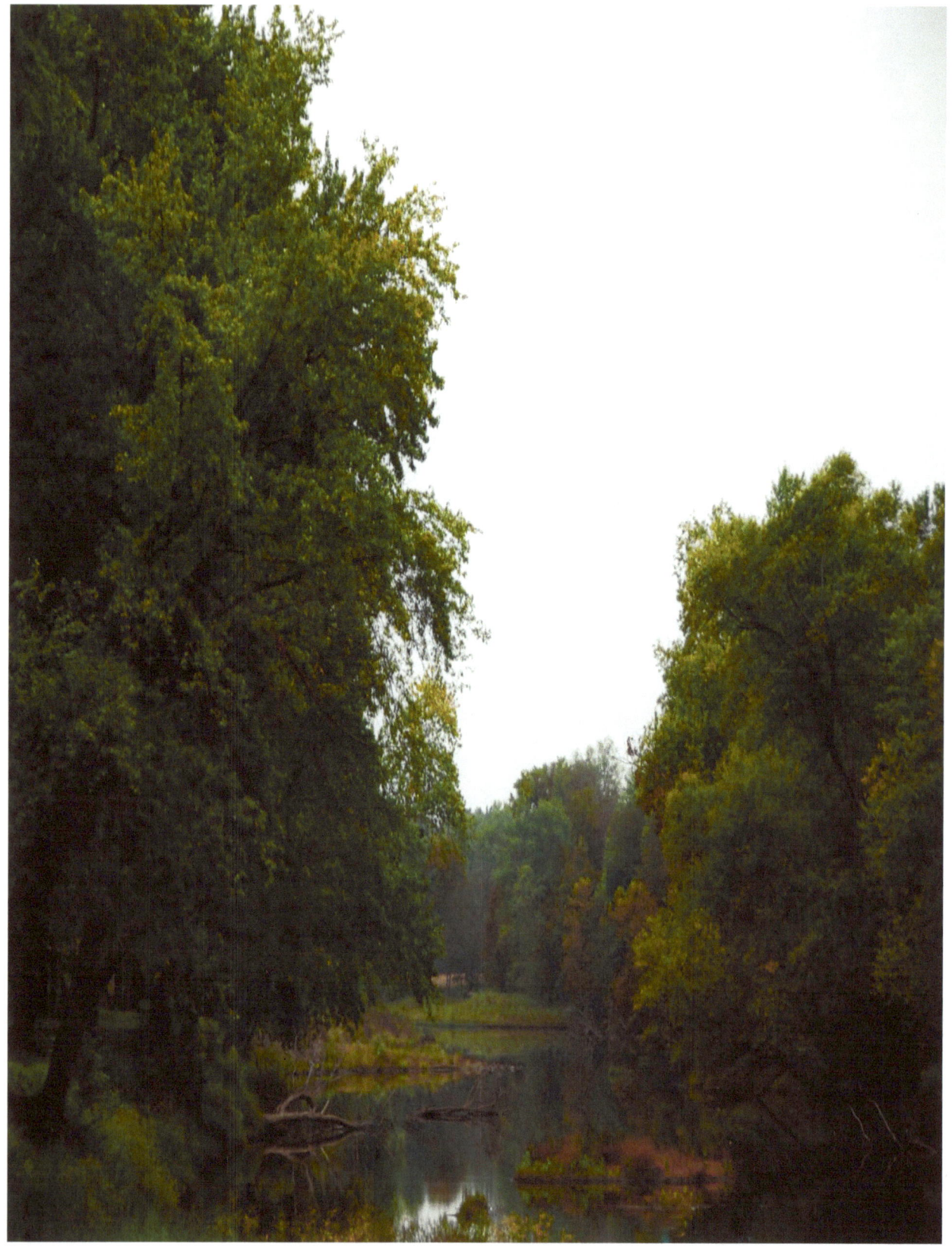

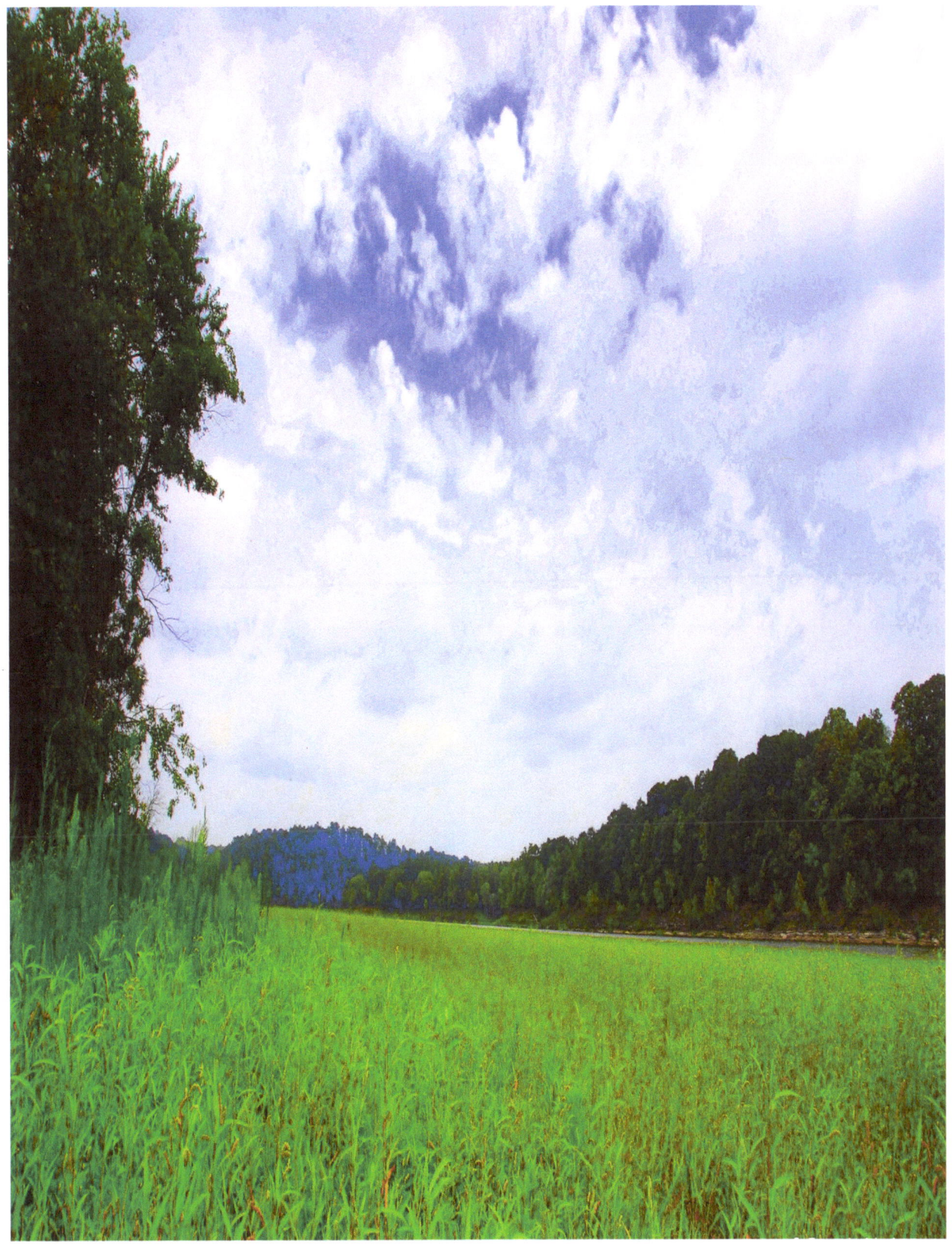

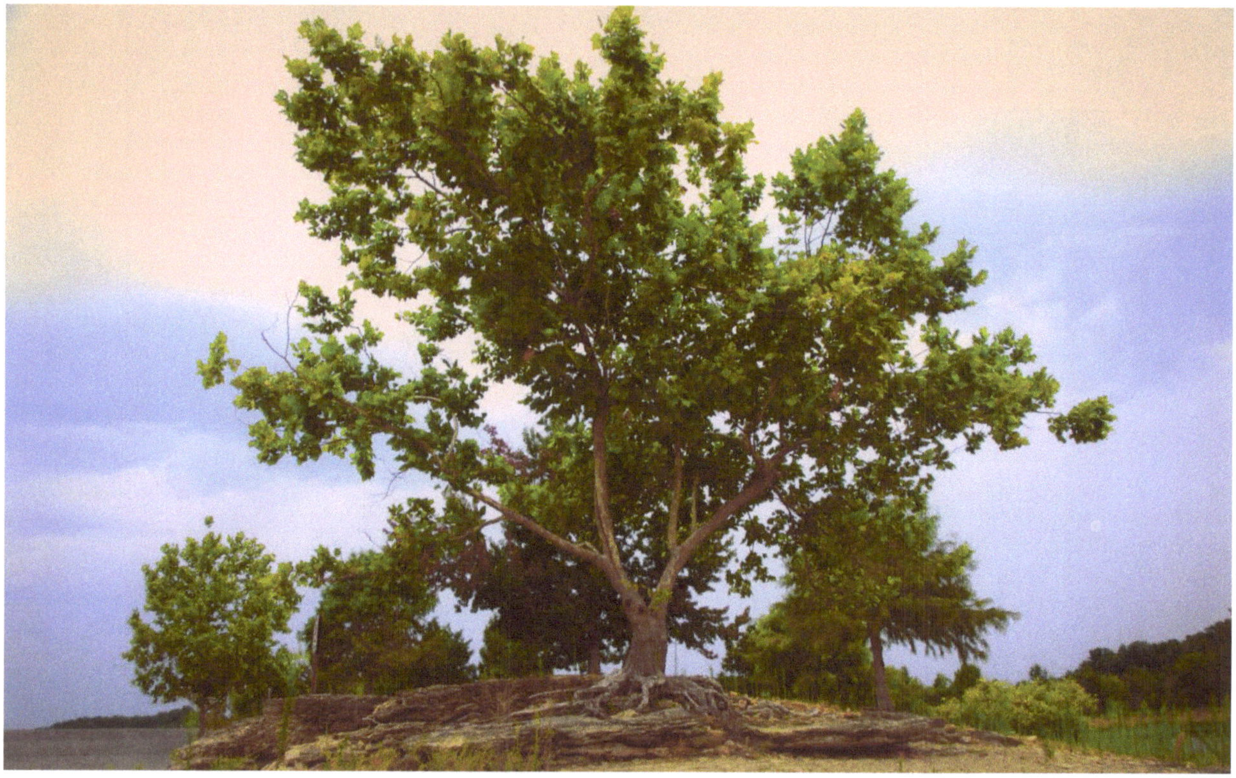

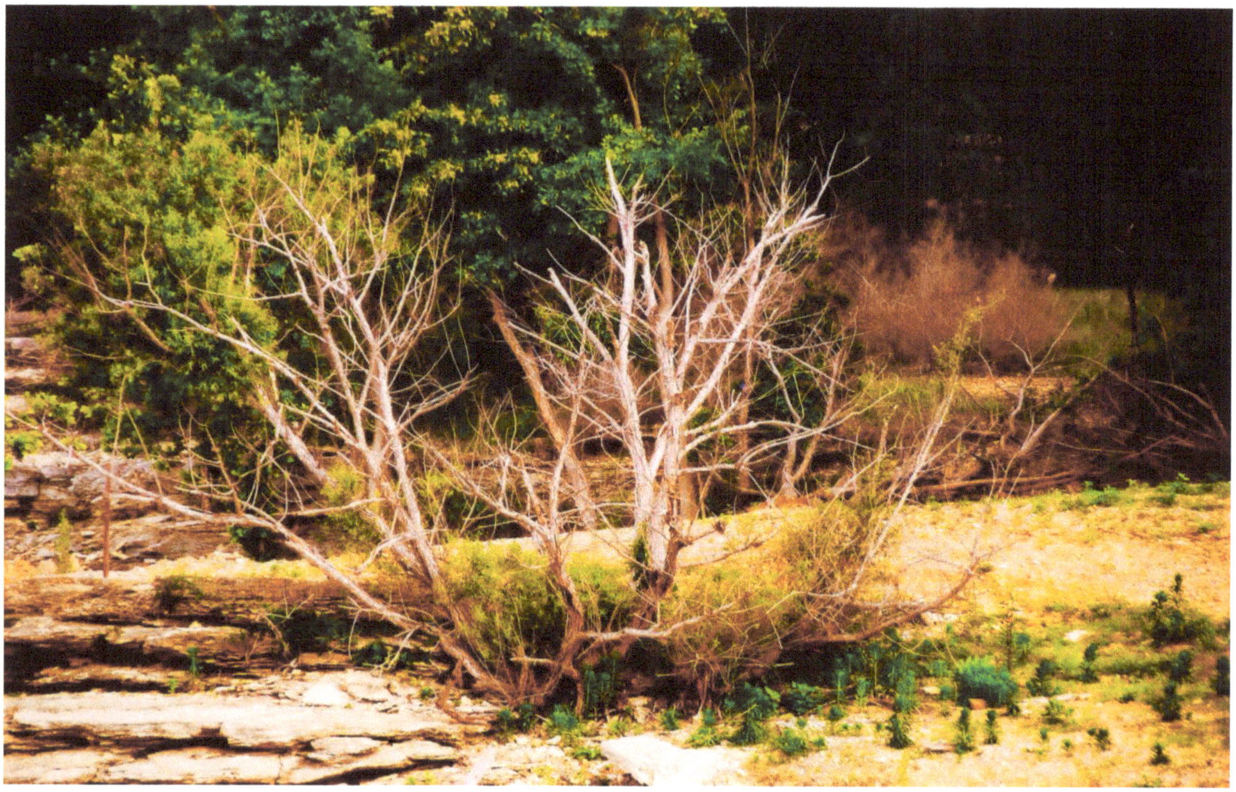

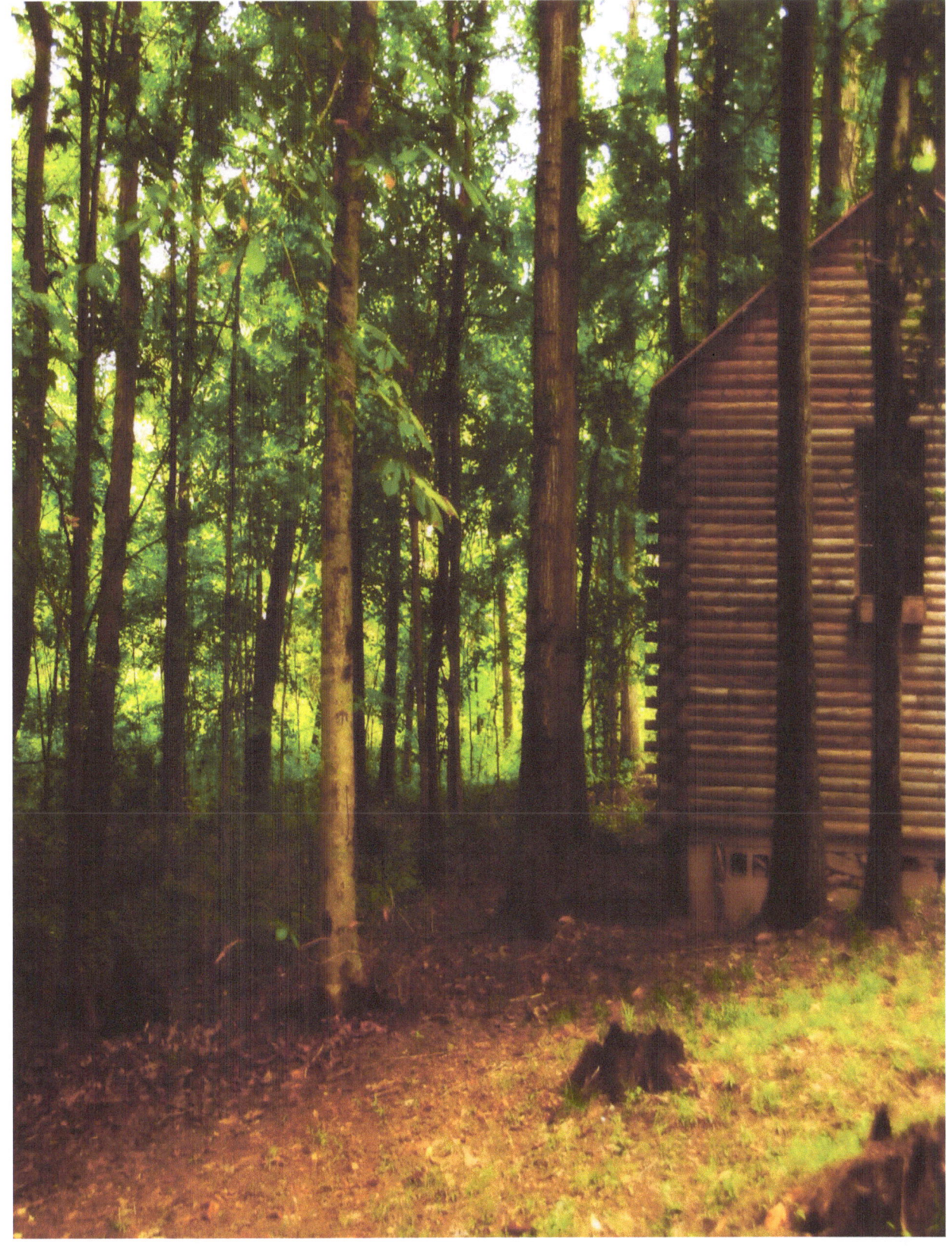

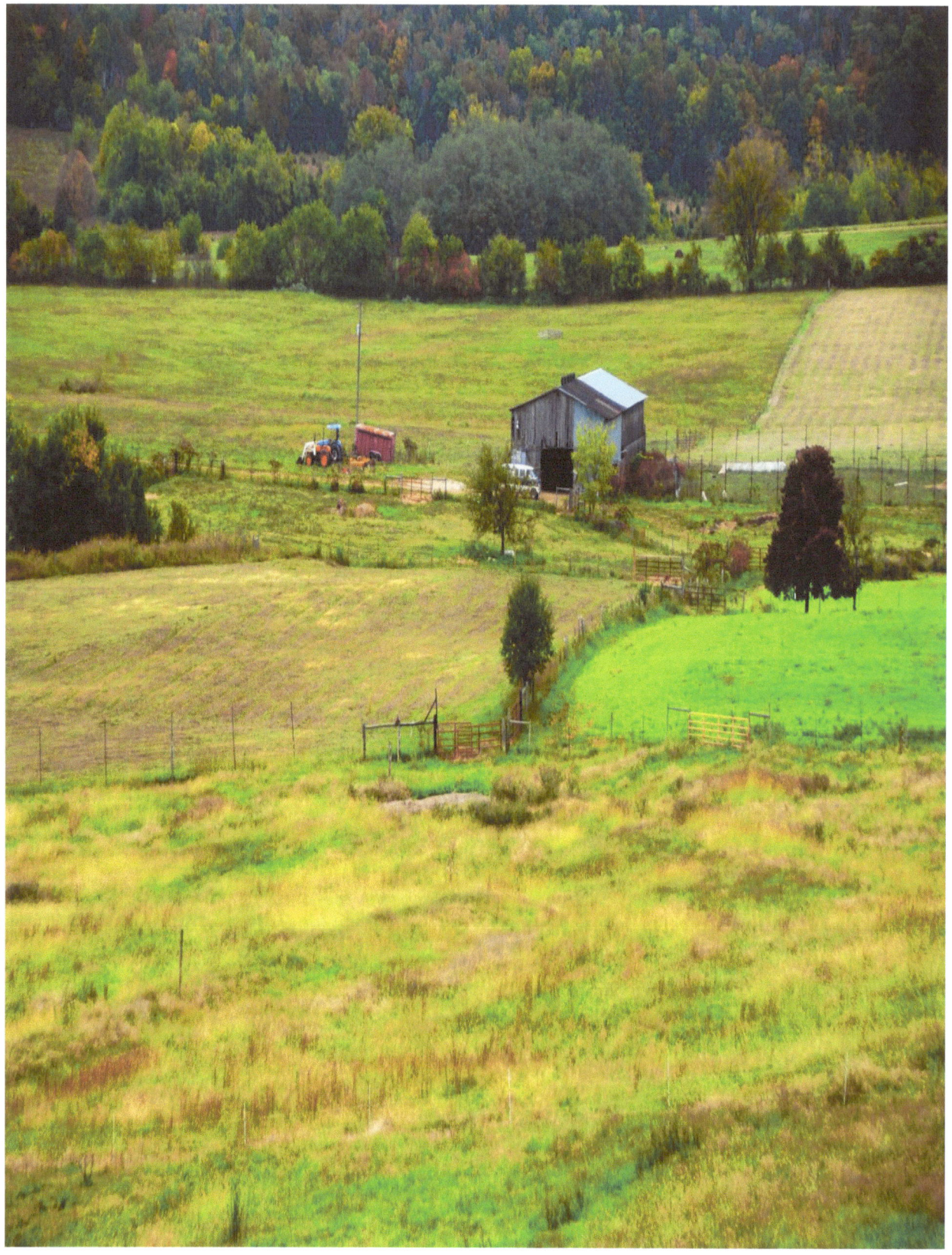

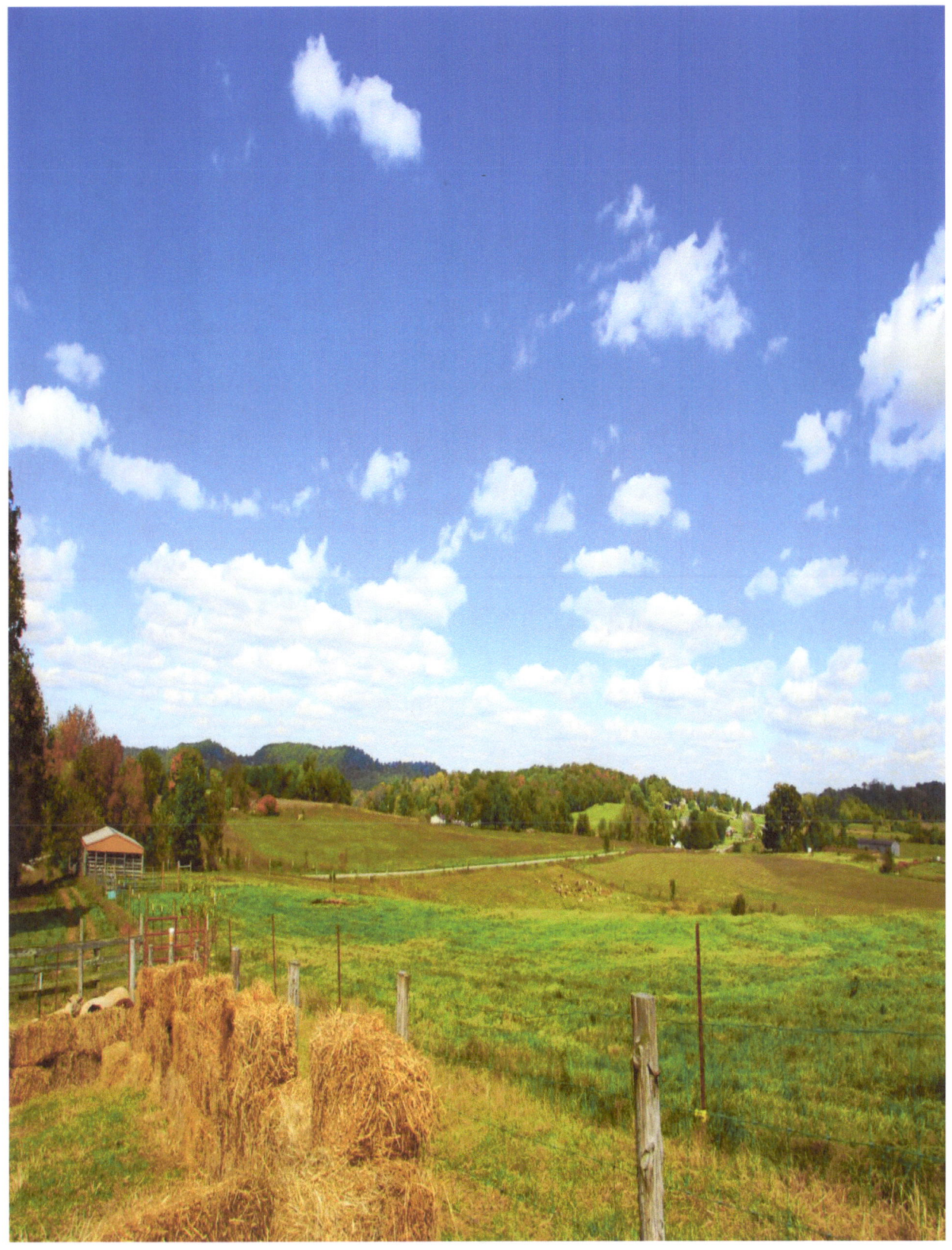

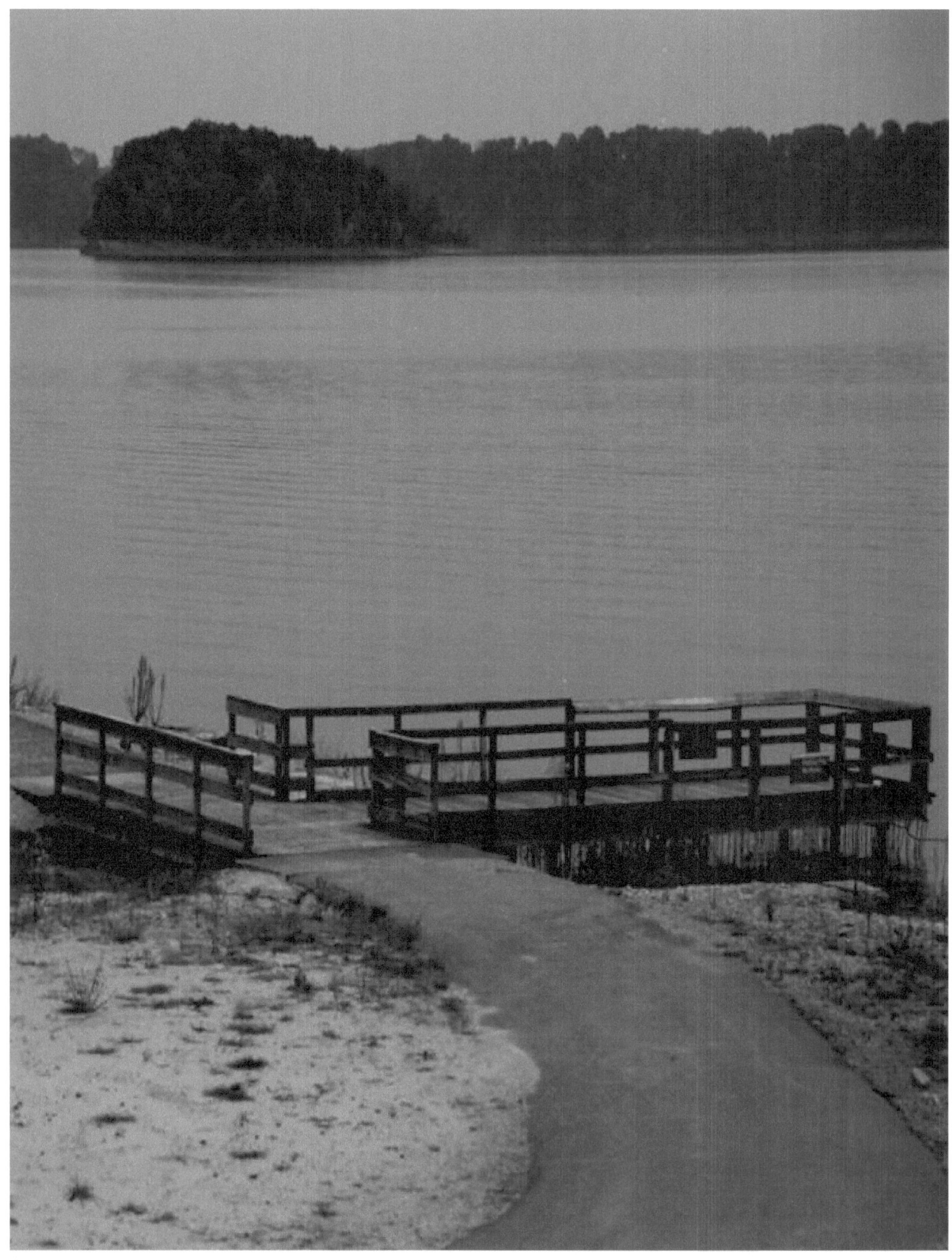

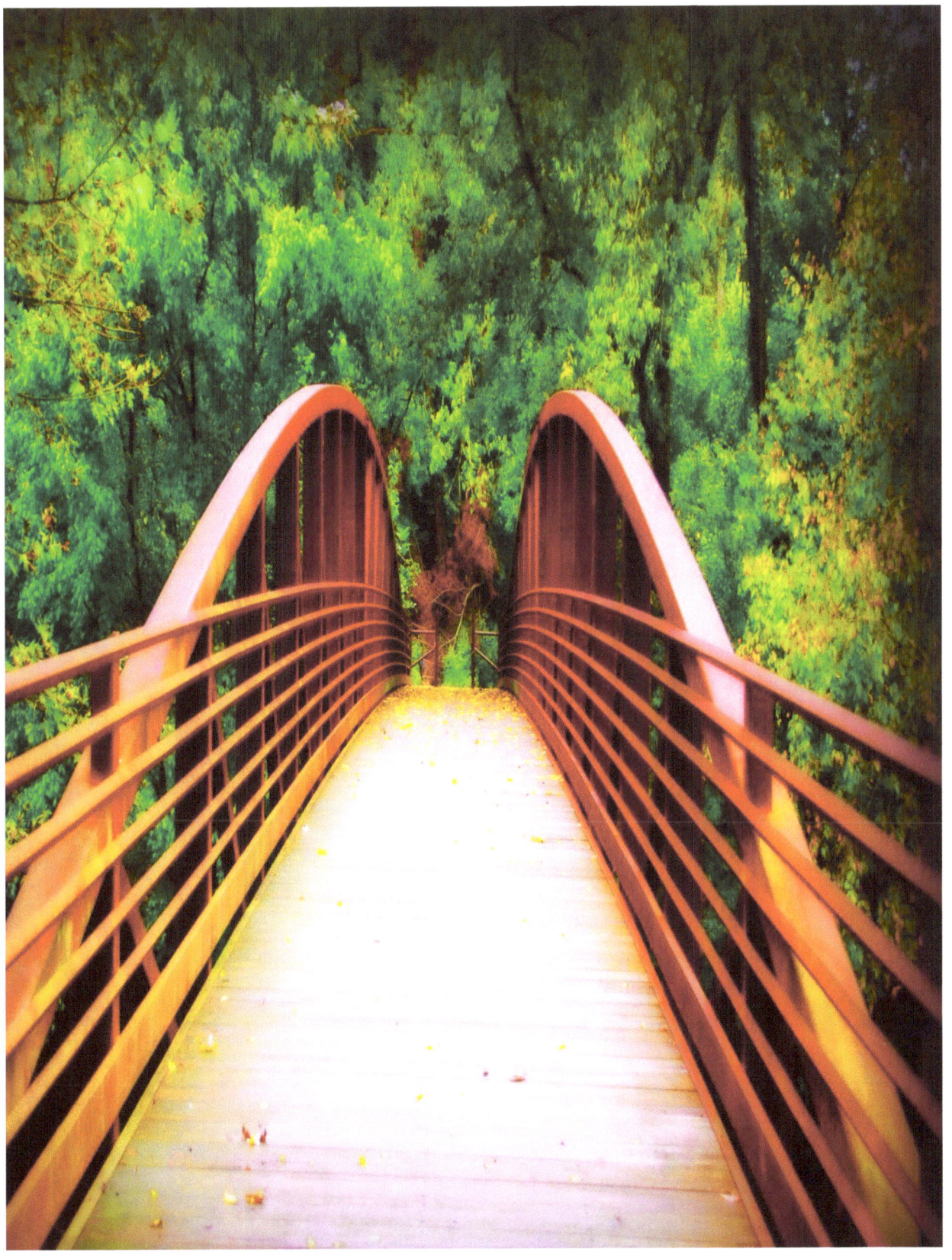

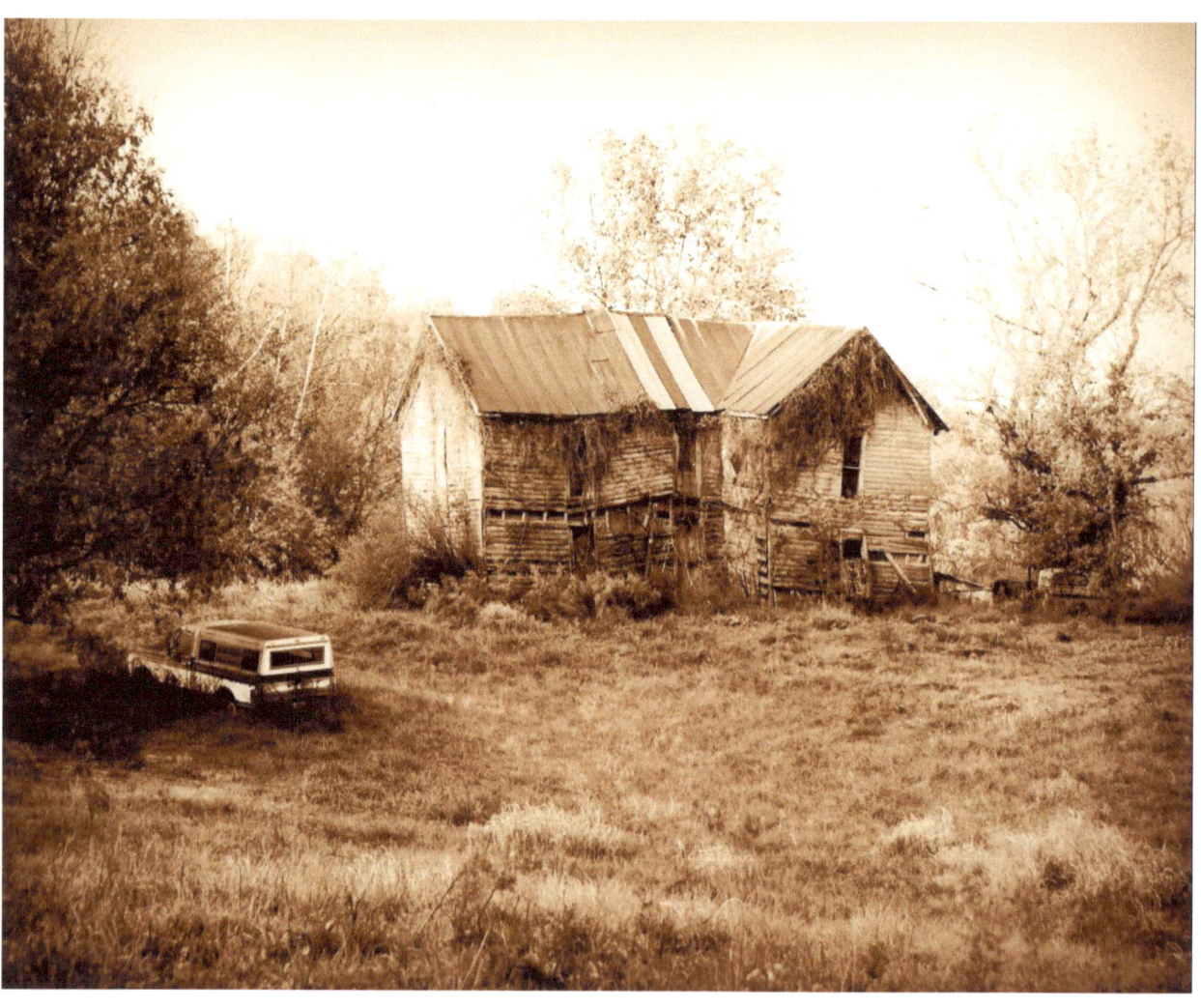

Lovely Creatures

Show kindness to animals also, as well as to all people. For as you treat all other created beings, so will you, in the long run, be treated.

Apocrypha, Text of The Twelve Fathers

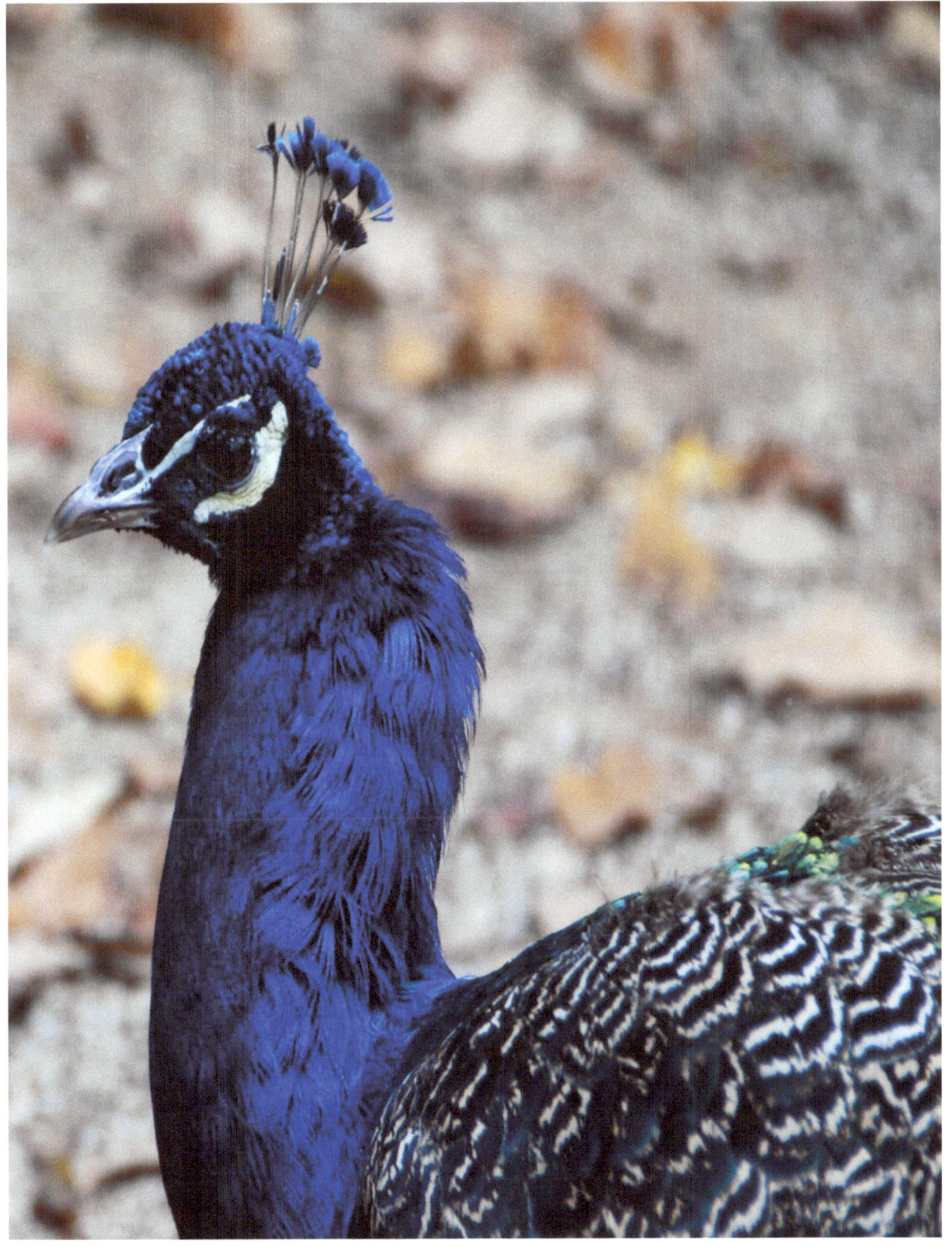

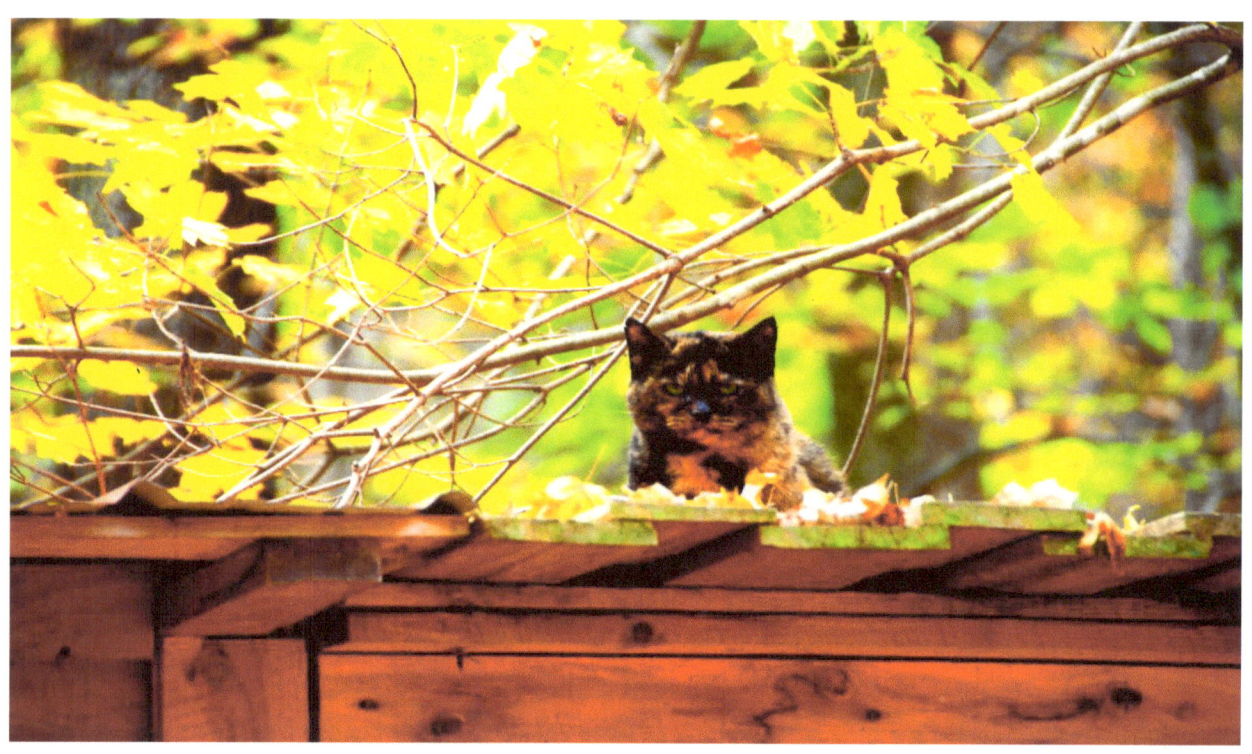

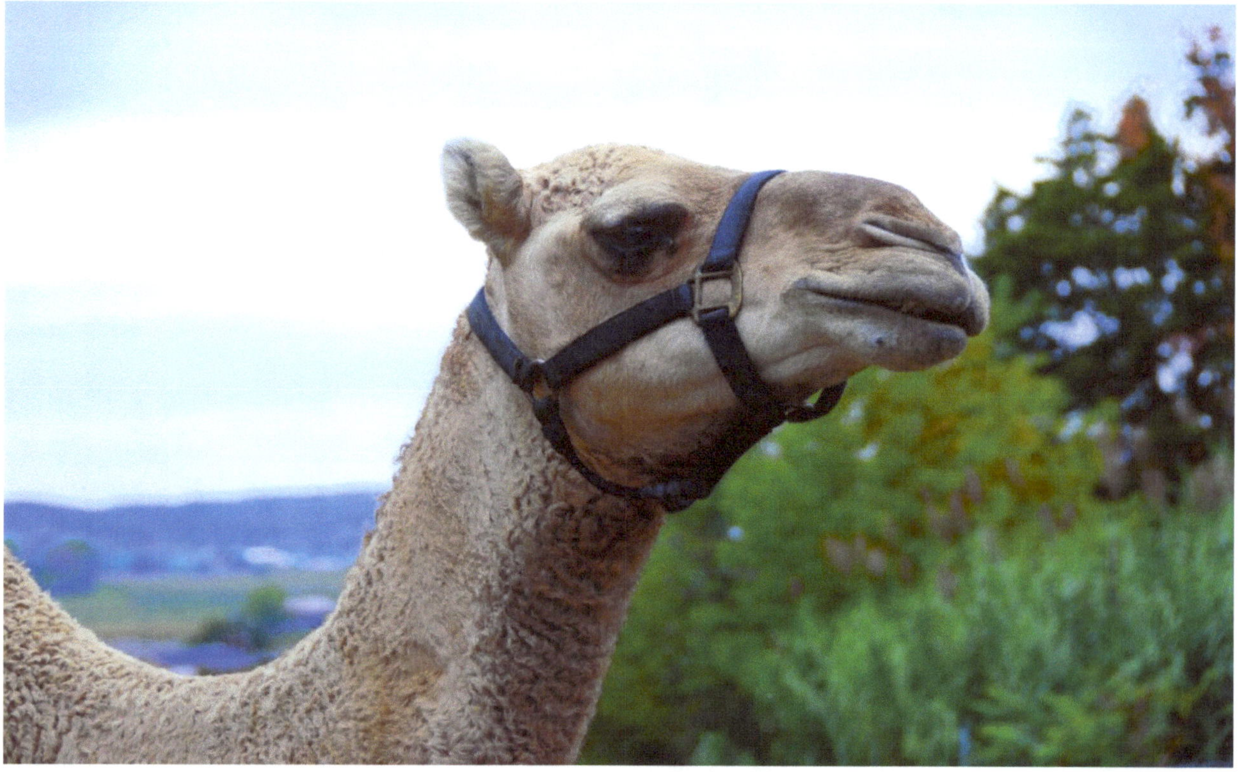

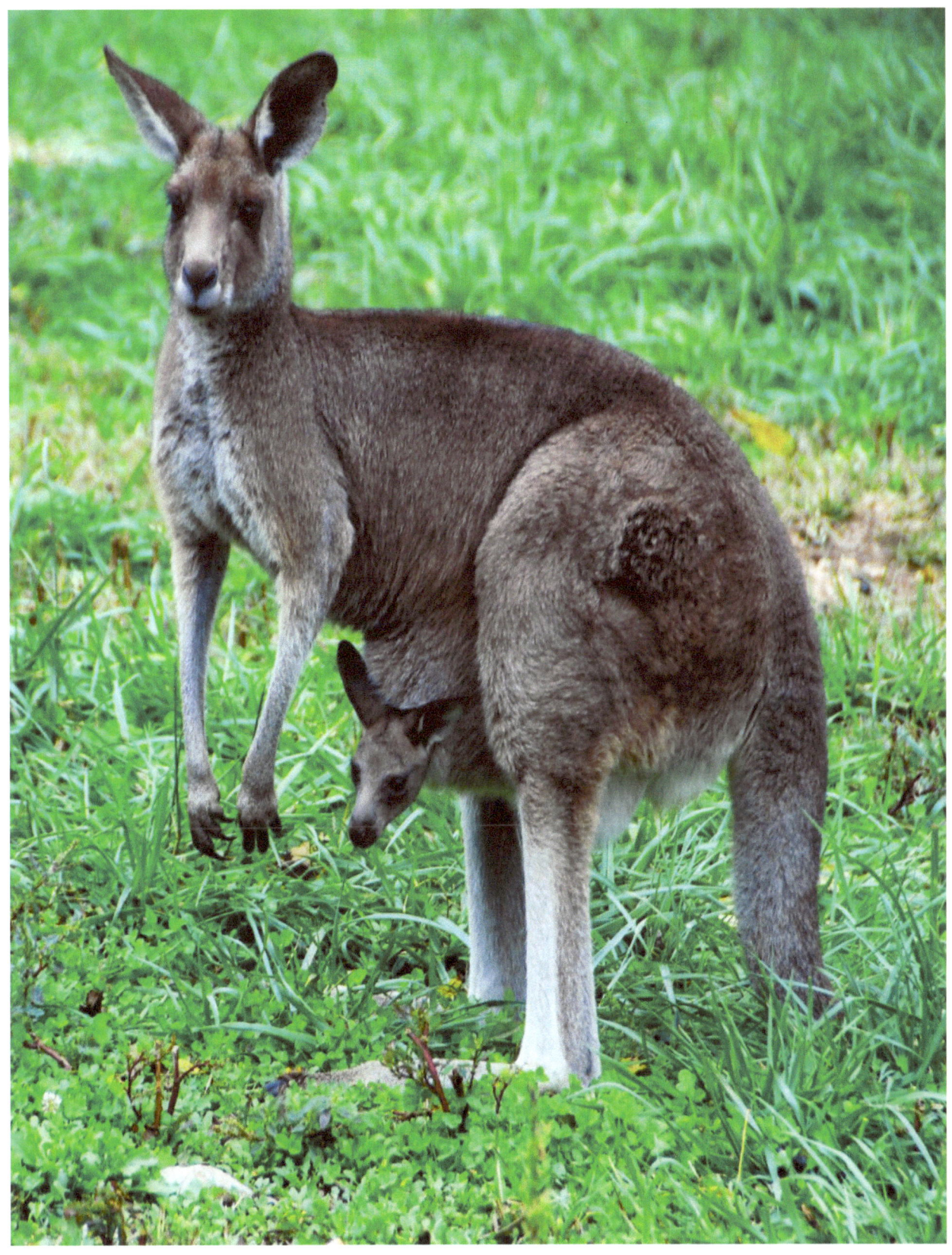

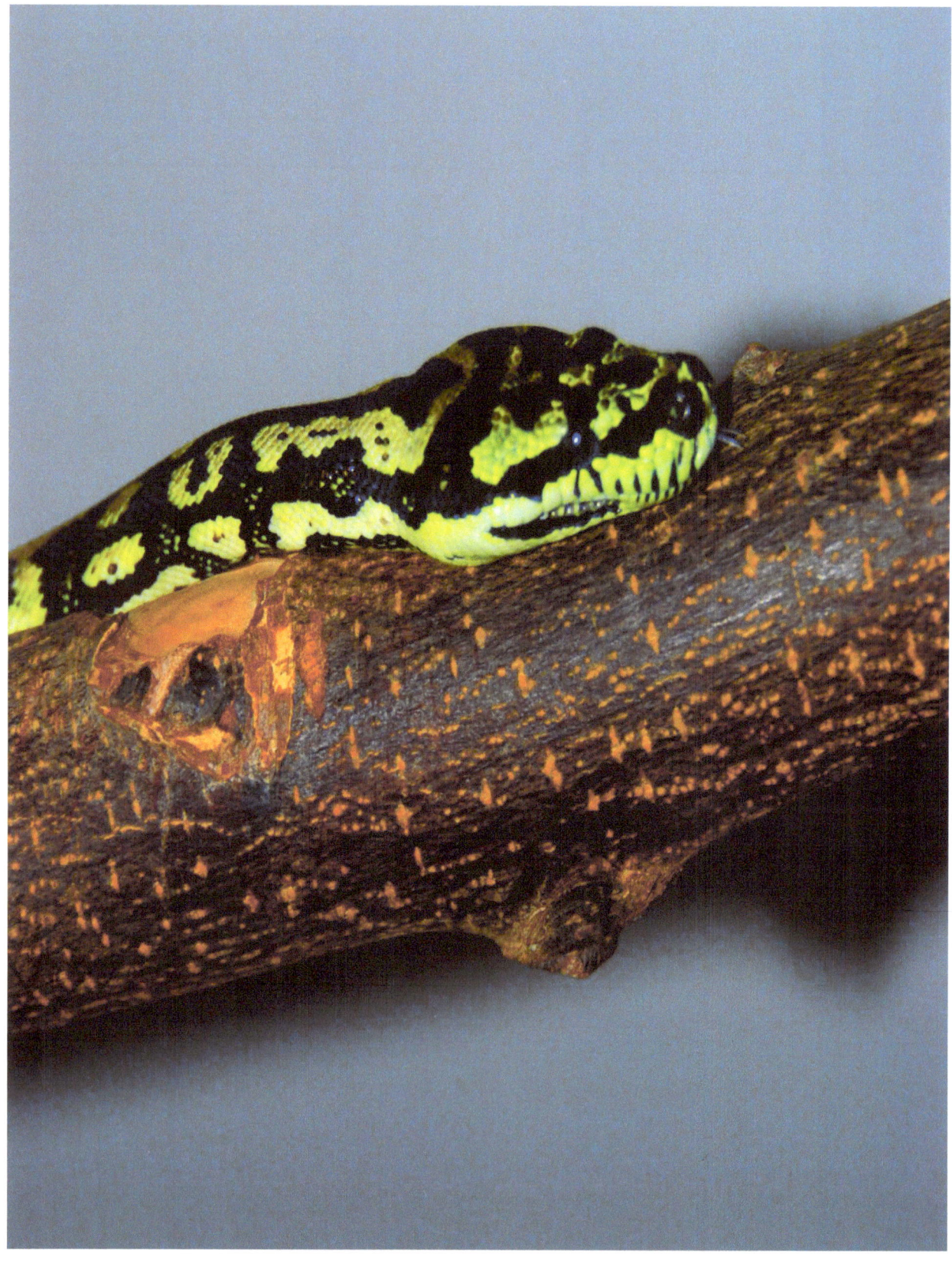

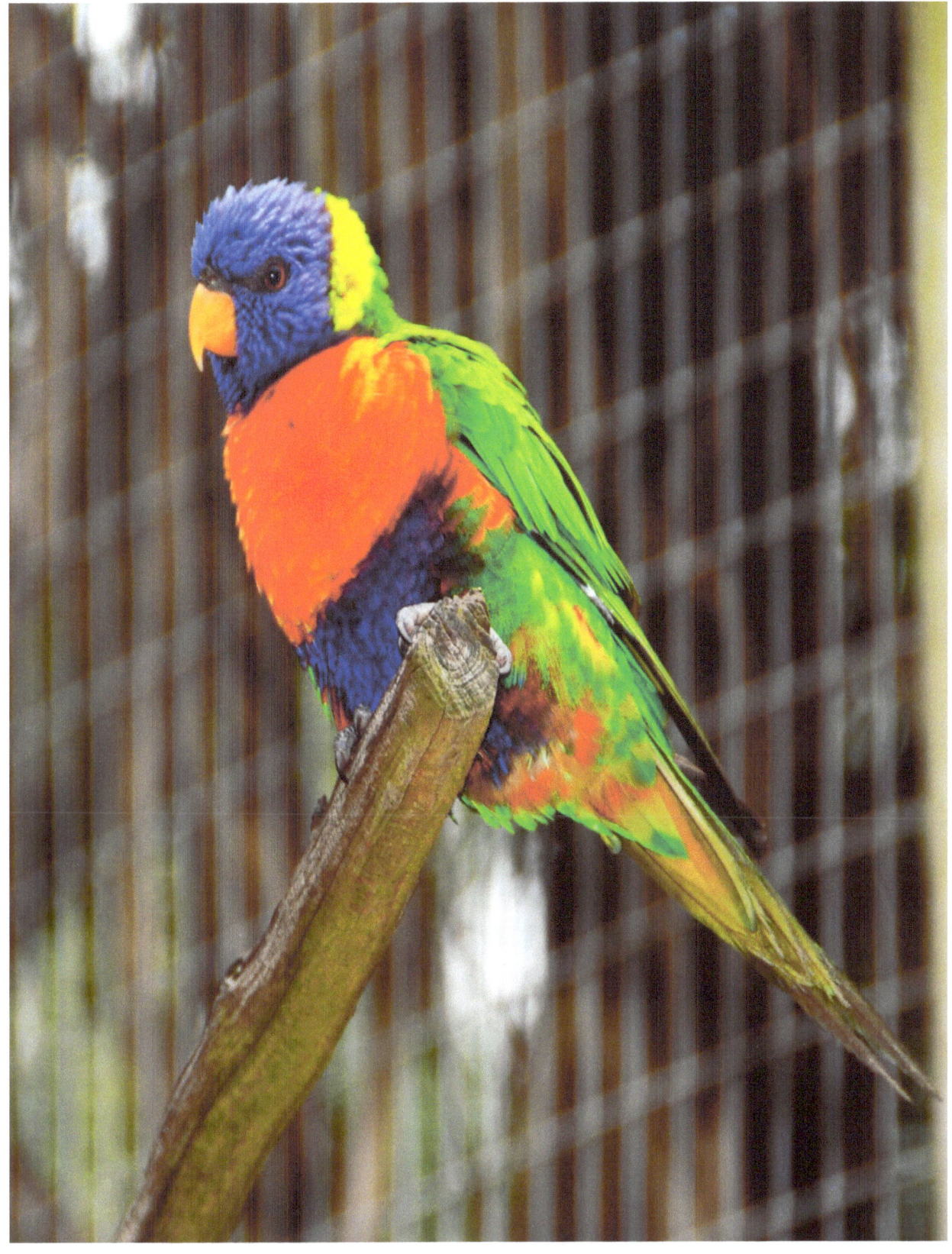

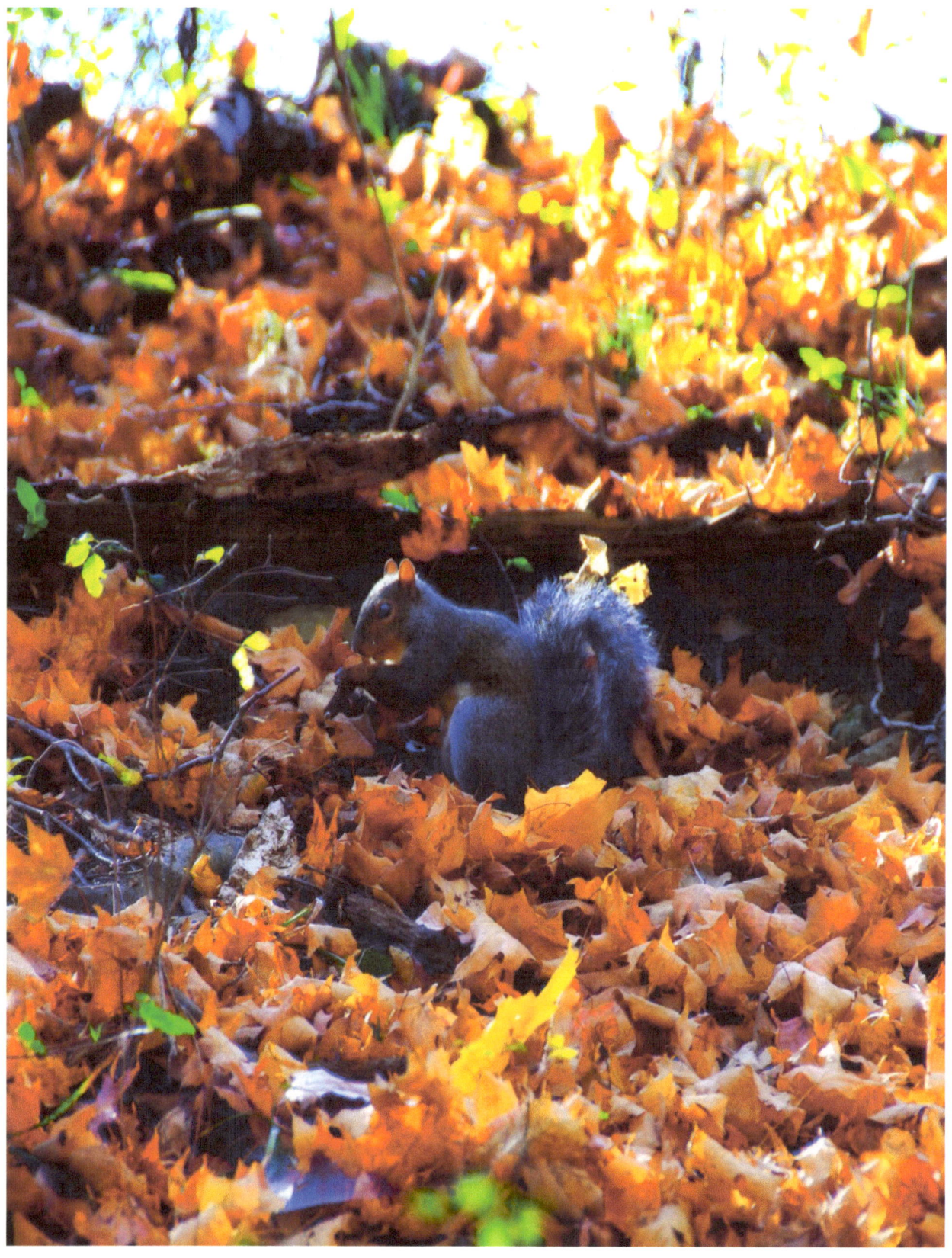

El Pescado

Because I could not stop for Death,
He kindly stopped for me;
The carriage held but just ourselves
And Immortality.

We slowly drove, he knew no haste,
And I had put away
My labour, and my leisure too,
For his civility.

We passed the school where children played,
Their lessons scarcely done;
We passed the fields of gazing grain,
We passed the setting sun.

We paused before a house that seemed
A swelling of the ground;
The roof was scarcely visible,
The cornice but a mound.

Since then 'tis centuries; but each
Feels shorter than the day
I first surmised the horses' heads
Were toward eternity

Emily Dickinson

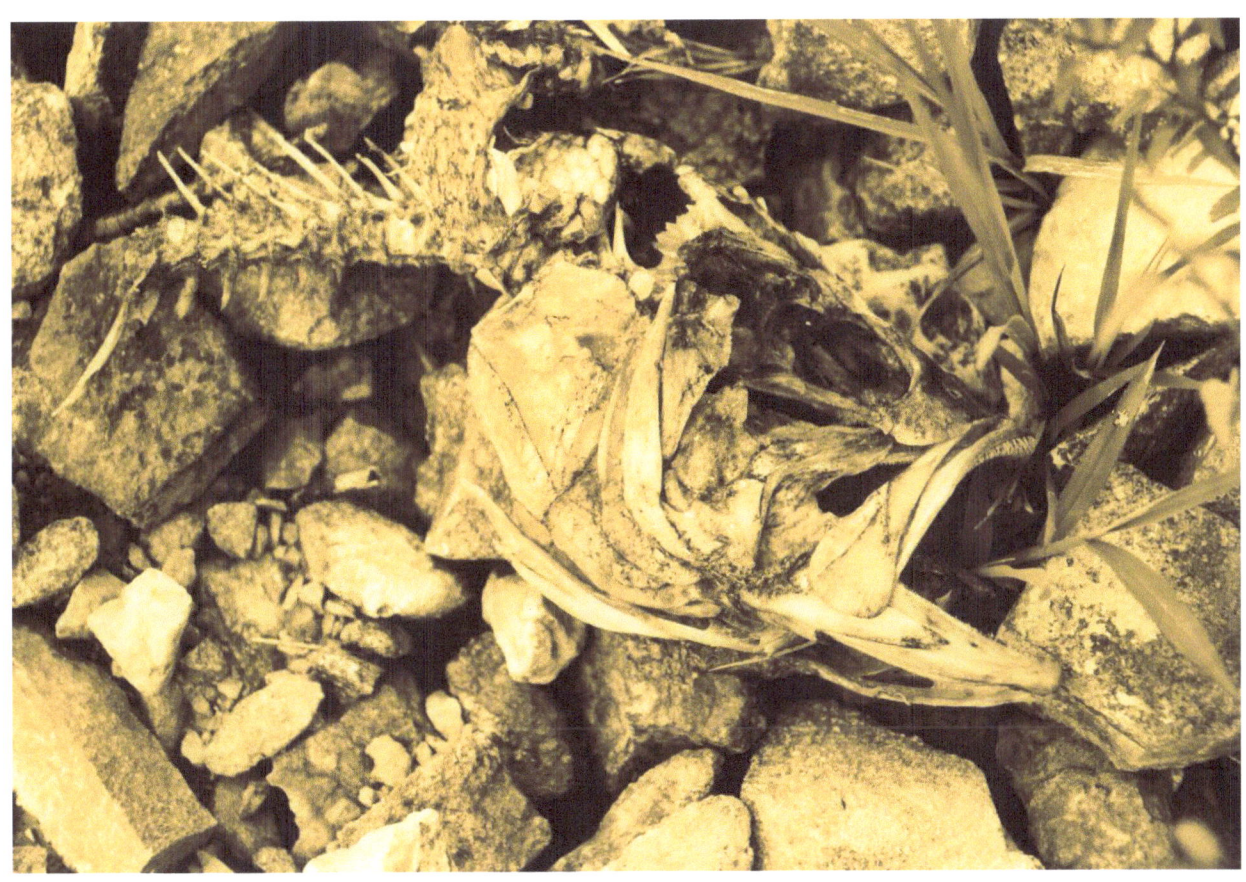

Author's Note

This book initially started out as simply a fall foliage book. I found it difficult to stick to just one theme since there was so much I wanted to include. I instead decided to fill a book with images that I felt were beautiful. Many of the landscape and animal photos were taken at Kentucky Down Under in Horse Cave, Kentucky. The shot with the sun coming through the trees was taken at Mammoth Cave National Park. The waterfall shots were taken at Burgess Falls in Sparta, Tennessee. The remainder were taken at areas throughout South Central Kentucky, Barren River Lake and Clarksville, Tennessee, and last but certainly not least my beautiful human subject is William Paul Carter.

I see beauty in everything. Sometimes the obvious, like the photos of the landscapes, the animals, my dear friend Paul, and sometimes the not so obvious, like an old abandoned house or the last photograph I included in the book. I came across those fish bones on a photo shoot several months ago. They stuck out to me and I took the shot. It is surprisingly one of my best sellers. What may strike some as grotesque can actually be a work of art to others. Who is to say what is le beau ideal? Beauty is in the eye of the beholder after all.

Brandy Lindsey

ABOUT THE AUTHOR

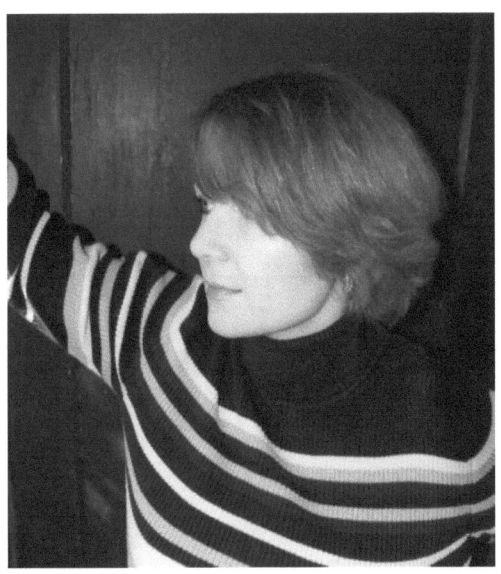

Brandy Lindsey is a freelance photographer who works out of the Kentucky and Tennessee areas. She primarily focuses on nature and landscape photography. Antiques are another one of her passions. When not out taking photos she is usually searching estate sales for treasures that she can restore for others to enjoy.
www.brandylindsey.com

www.ingramcontent.com/pod-product-compliance
Lightning Source LLC
Chambersburg PA
CBHW050758180526
45159CB00003B/1501